MW01071378

Single Mothers Speak on Patriarchy

a Girl God Anthology

Edited by Trista Hendren

& Pat Daly

Cover Art by Liz Darling

"And you will be like God..."

ISBN 9781537564647

www.thegirlgod.com

Praise for Single Mothers Speak on Patriarchy

"If we are ever to value women, we must value mothers. Our voices can be easily ignored or dismissed. *Single Mothers Speak on Patriarchy* raises the voices of women who are so easily dismissed. This collection of words and art from single mothers is at once enraging, inspiring, uncomfortable, moving and authentic. Solidarity, sisters, and congratulations on speaking your truth. The rest of us? Listen up. #MothersOfTheWorldUnite."
-Vanessa Olorenshaw, author of *Liberating Motherhood*

"These are voices that need to be heard ... yet so many block their ears: the pain of memory and/or recognition may be too much. These stories speak a deep essential truth about the global cultural context for those engaged in maternal care, and where lies the illnesses of our times - that are seen played out everyday...This anthology furthers and encourages the speaking of womens' truths, which often does indeed split the world open: but it apparently needs to be so. May more have the courage required, and may they be safer as they do so. May those who hear have more compassionate response for the mothers and the children, and may laws be enacted as if She – in us all – mattered."
-Glenys Livingstone Ph.D., author of *PaGaian Cosmology*

"This book was a wake-up call, a look at things from the perspective of women, single mothers, who have been unjustly treated by a patriarchal society. The book is filled with stories from around the world, but one uniting thread binds them all together and that is strength. I encourage everyone to read this book."
-Amanda Evans, author of *Surviving Suicide*

Girl God Books

Original Resistance: Reclaiming Lilith, Reclaiming Ourselves
There is, perhaps, no more powerful archetype of female resistance than Lilith. As women across the globe rise up against the patriarchy, Lilith stands beside them, misogyny's original challenger. This anthology—a chorus of voices hitting chords of defiance, liberation, anger and joy—reclaims the goodness of women bold enough to hold tight to their essence. Through poetry, prose, incantation, prayer and imagery, women from all walks of life invite you to join them in the revolutionary act of claiming their place—of reclaiming themselves.

Inanna's Ascent: Reclaiming Female Power
Inanna's Ascent examines how females can rise from the underworld and reclaim their power, sovereignly expressed through poetry, prose and visual art. All contributors are extraordinary women in their own right, who have been through some difficult life lessons—and are brave enough to share their stories.

Re-visioning Medusa: from Monster to Divine Wisdom
A remarkable collection of essays, poems, and art: by scholars who have researched Her, artists who have envisioned Her, women who have known Her in their personal story, and then also combinations of all those capacities. All have spoken with Her and share something of their communion in this anthology.

Jesus, Muhammad and the Goddess
More than 35 international contributors reflect on finding Goddess within (and without) Christianity and Islam.

New Love: a reprogramming toolbox for undoing the knots

A powerful combination of emotional/spiritual techniques, art and inspiring words for women who wish to move away from patriarchal thought. This reprogramming toolbox combines the wisdom of intentional visual art and inspiring words. *New Love* includes a mixture of compelling thoughts and suggestions for each day, along with a "toolbox" to help you change the parts of your life you want to heal.

THE CREATIVE WARRIOR: A Colouring Journal for Adults to Awaken the Creative Child

So much more than an ordinary colouring book; *The Creative Warrior* is a journey of personal empowerment. This book has been designed to awaken your inner creative being and gently connect you with your most satisfying and creative self. *The Creative Warrior* blossoms with encouraging quotes, numerous colouring sheets of unique images, suggestions, activities and insightful thoughts. Written and illustrated by Arna Baartz.

Hearts Aren't Made of Glass

My Journey from Princess of Nothing to Goddess of My Own Damned Life. By Trista Hendren.

How to Live Well Despite Capitalist Patriarchy

A book challenging societal assumptions to help women become stronger and break free of their chains.

The Girl God

A book for children young and old, celebrating the Divine Feminine. Magically illustrated by Elisabeth Slettnes with quotes from various faith traditions and feminist thinkers.

See a complete list at thegirlgod.com

"The genius of any slave system is found in the
dynamics which isolate slaves from each other,
obscure the reality of a common condition,
and make united rebellion against
the oppressor inconceivable."

-Andrea Dworkin

Table of Contents

"Women have been driven mad, 'gaslighted,' for centuries by the refutation of our experience and our instincts in a culture which validates only male experience. The truth of our bodies and our minds has been mystified to us.

We therefore have a primary obligation to each other: not to undermine each other's sense of reality for the sake of expediency; not to gaslight each other.

Women have often felt insane when cleaving to the truth of our experience.

Our future depends on the sanity of each of us, and we have a profound stake, beyond the personal, in the project of describing our reality as candidly and fully as we can to each other.

When a woman tells the truth she is creating the possibility for more truth around her."

-Adrienne Rich, *On Lies, Secrets, and Silence*

Introduction
Trista Hendren

Many people have wondered why I am going off track with my Goddess work to write about single mothers. To me, *it's all related.*

The way we treat mothers is indicative of how we view The Mother.

> *"Under patriarchy, the mother is feared and hated, quite crazily, both for her power and her weakness; everything a man cannot courageously accept about himself is projected onto his mother, or wife."*
> *–Monica Sjoo & Barbara Mor[1]*

To me, honoring *real life* mothers is just as important as setting aside our indoctrination to believe in a male God.

As someone who has been both a married mother and a single mother, I can tell you that there is a big difference in the way the world treats you. There is also an enormous difference as to what your perceived "rights" are: namely whether or not anyone else will help you—financially or otherwise—to raise your children.

It's hard to feel like a Goddess when you're worried sick about how you are going to feed your kids. You can do all the affirmations and self-help work you want, but it is a rare woman who feels empowered living in poverty.

---

1 Sjoo, Monica and Mor, Barbara. *The Great Cosmic Mother.* HarperOne. 1987.

Amy Logan wrote in *The Seven Perfumes of Sacrifice*, "Every time they butcher a woman for honor, they're killing the Goddess."[2] I believe that is true with every rape and murder of a female, and to a somewhat lesser extent, every time a woman is hit, verbally abused or forced to live in poverty.

Putting this anthology together was quite upsetting at times. Reading through the submissions of other single moms often was rather devastating. I felt overwhelmed by the task of changing a system that is so globally entrenched. I was often disappointed with the lack of response from other feminists—who had, perhaps never been in these shoes themselves.

Many of us don't aspire to be single mothers. I sure didn't. The first time around, I became pregnant fairly early into a new relationship with a man I was crazy about. I was not aware at the time that the father of my child had struggled with addiction since his teen years. After more than a year of being a single mom and struggling alone, the father of my child went to an extended rehab and became sober.

After a year of maintaining his sobriety, I married him. I felt ecstatic. I was sure my misery and difficult years were over. I excelled at my career and lived a fairly affluent lifestyle while both of us were working. We had another child—and, a year later, he relapsed.

I wasn't expecting to find cocaine in my home. I wasn't expecting another extended rehab that did not take. I wasn't expecting that I would have to continue paying bills on one income while caring for two young children alone. We lived in a nice home and belonged to a country club. My children attended private schools

---

2 Logan, Amy. *The Seven Perfumes of Sacrifice*. Priya Press. 2012.

and were enrolled in every sort of extracurricular activity imaginable.

Initially I received about 10% of our annual budget in child support and alimony. Needless to say, that did not begin to cover our expenses. In the years that followed, I divorced, filed for bankruptcy and lost my home.

I often say that I will never fully recover from my years as a single mom. Sadly, this is true for many of us, although it need not be.

I may have left my status of "single mother" behind several years ago when I remarried, but the repercussions of those years have still followed me. I still have no retirement fund saved for my later years due to the three accounts I had to cash out to feed my children. My credit is still ruined and I have nothing in savings. My back and neck are still in chronic pain every day—a leftover from the tremendous stress of those years—and I do not have the funds to do much about it.

You don't just *recover* from being a single mother. You *deal with it* the best way you can.

I received hundreds of inquiries for this anthology, and few of them told a happy story.

The thing is, when you're isolated as a single mom, you believe you are the only one going through all this. As Andrea Dworkin wrote, "The genius of any slave system is found in the dynamics which isolate slaves from each other, obscure the reality of a common condition, and make united rebellion against the oppressor inconceivable."

Years of participation in a single mothers' group has shown me that although we may *feel* alone, we certainly are *not* alone in numbers or our experiences. I believe it is time for women to stop suffering in silence and tell our stories so that we can change this dynamic. As James Baldwin once wrote:

> *"The victim who is able to articulate the situation*
> *of the victim has ceased to be a victim: he or she*
> *has become a threat."*

I tell more of my personal story in *Hearts Aren't Made of Glass*[3]. However, my connections with women in similar situations over the last 13 years convinced me that we needed a collection of stories. We must reveal the worldwide scale of abuse toward single mothers. It is not just individual men who are doing this; it is our laws and lack of understanding around this issue that allow it to continue on such a large scale.

At the time of publication, I am owed more than $46,000 in past due court-ordered child support, but no one—at the state or national level—seems interested enforcing that child support. I racked up another $22,000+ in legal fees in Family Court, that my ex was ultimately ordered to pay by the judge—but no one is enforcing that either.

In the U.S. alone, there is more than $108 billion of unpaid child support.[4]

---

3 Hendren, Trista. *Hearts Aren't Made of Glass: My Journey from Princess of Nothing to Goddess of My Own Damned Life*. Girl God Press. 2016.
4 Hargreaves, Steve. "Deadbeat parents cost taxpayers $53 billion." *CNN/Money.* November 5, 2012.

In her study of Women and Poverty, Marielena Zuniga notes that, "In 2007, only 31 percent of female-headed families in the U.S. reported receiving child support payments during the previous year." [5]

I don't have a collective number on legal fees worldwide, but in talking to other women, I know I am not alone in this either. Men are successfully using the "Family Court" systems to tank us. This is particularly troubling when you look at how much women give of themselves to care for their children.

As Vanessa Olorenshaw writes in *Liberating Motherhood,* "When it comes to *women*, how far do patriarchal and exploitative capitalist values *rely* on women providing *unwaged* care, on which our society can freeload and from which it can wash its hands of financial responsibility?"[6]

So often, we are told to just suck it up—for the sake of our children. The only group that our silence helps are the men who don't do their part—and the agencies who allow them to get away with it.

We are not *less strong* for admitting how terribly hard and inhumane it feels to be single mothers. We are shining the light on an important human rights violation—and allowing other women to do the same. We are demanding better lives for ourselves and our children.

$108 billion is not a *small* problem. And it doesn't begin to measure the long-term effects on women and children. As far as I

5 Zuniga, Marielena. "Women & Poverty." Revised September 2011.
http://www.soroptimist.org/whitepapers/whitepaperdocs/wpwomenpoverty.pdf
6 Orenshaw, Vanessa. *Liberating Motherhood: Birthing the Purplestockings Movement.* Womancraft Publishing. 2016.

know, no one has calculated the worldwide total of unpaid child support either—but I would guess it is somewhere in the trillions. As Ann Crittenden writes, "A society which beggars its mothers beggars its own future."

As we were finishing this book, I happened upon the documentary, "The True Cost." There I learned the story of Shima—a single mother in Bangladesh who is one of 40 million garment workers around the world. I was heartbroken to hear her story of making approximately three dollars a day while caring for her young daughter alone. Sometimes she would bring her daughter to the factory with her, but the chemicals were harmful for her young body and she had no one to help care for her. Ultimately, she had to leave her young daughter in the care of her parents outside the city—for about a year at a time—to provide her daughter with a better life.

No mother should have to make this sort of sacrifice. If women in Western countries are suffering as single mothers, it is logical that women in poorer countries suffer even more. This is a global problem that this anthology is just scratching the surface of. As Zuniga notes:

> "Nearly one-third of all households worldwide are headed by women. In certain parts of Africa and Latin America, as many as 45 percent of households are female-headed."[7]

I had hoped to include more stories from women like Shima in this book. However, just the ability to write your story connotes some amount of privilege. Throughout the period of collecting stories for this anthology, I was met with a similar response. Women

---

7 Zuniga, Marielena. "Women & Poverty." Revised September 2011.

wanted—often desperately—to tell their stories, but lacked the time to be able to sit down and tell them.

Furthermore, there are many parts of the world where educating girls is not a priority—and it is painfully obvious that those women and their stories are often not heard at all—at least in print.

We have included many voices of women who are not native English speakers in this anthology. However because this project was self-funded, we lacked the ability to track down and translate stories of women who did not speak English at all.

Sadly, as someone who is still suffering financially from my own years as a single mom, I did not have the time or the resources to carry out this project all the way.

This anthology is meant to be a starting point—which hopefully will inspire others to carry on this work and make radical changes for single mothers and their children.

I hope other single moms will join us in shedding the secrecy and shame around this issue. My vision is that other women will join their sisters in demanding fair treatment. *All* of our children deserve to grow up surrounded by love and peace—not pain, poverty and stress.

A Note About Styles and Preferences

Single Mothers Speak on Patriarchy contains a variety of writing styles from women around the world. Non-English natives and various forms of English are included in this anthology and we chose to keep spellings of the writers' place of origin to honor (or honour) each woman's unique voice.

It was the expressed intent of the editors to not police standards of citation, transliteration and formatting. Contributors have determined which citation style, italicization policy and transliteration system to adopt in their pieces. The resulting diversity is a reflection of the diversity of academic fields, genres and personal expressions represented by the authors.[8]

Please note that some contributors have chosen to write anonymously or with pen names—and some of those authors have also opted not to share their biography to further protect their anonymity. We have done our best to protect the names of women and their children—who may be in danger or face repercussions for speaking out. If you should recognize one of these women, please honor their anonymity.

---

8 This paragraph is borrowed and adapted with love from *A Jihad for Justice: Honoring the Work and Life of Amina Wadud* – Edited by Kecia Ali, Juliane Hammer and Laury Silvers.

Barely Escaping Within the Patriarchy

Beth Mattson

WHAT IS THE IMPALPABLE *SOMETHING* that looms over the otherwise blissful life of myself, a single mother, and my children? What is it that maintains my ex-husband's abusive voice in our daily lives? What is it that dictated an official child support formula that keeps me in food stamps while my ex-husband makes six figures a year? What is the factor that keeps my male employer, my kids' grandfather, or my young, often male students from fully appreciating how difficult it is to be an adjunct professor and a single mother? I often think it is patriarchy – this system of slightly favoring the unproven word or value of a man over a woman.

When my beautiful, genius, also-a-mama lawyer wrote a statement to our divorce case judge – mentioning that my now ex-husband had been fired thrice already, that he had no family in our then-current state of residence, that I had a stable job and family lined up in my home state – that judge granted me permission to leave the state of residence for my home state. But she didn't want to see the pictures of the mystery bruises and filth with which my children returned from their father's even brief care. I didn't get to testify that their father had once gotten drunk and locked me out, away from the baby, on purpose. We didn't get the time to mention that he cheated, was extremely unstable, and terrorized me through a campaign of forbidding change to the thermostat, opening windows, using certain kinds of silverware, and forbidding visits to family and friends. We didn't get a chance to mention that he tried to decline paying for childcare so that I couldn't get a job outside of the home, nor that he stopped putting money into the family checking account, even while he forced us to still live together.

But it is considered great, vast, massive, good fortune that a judge lets a mother with children leave the state in which the father resides, so we didn't push our luck. We couldn't when we tried. The judge told my lawyer to "go away with that" – referring to the picture of my four-year-old with a large bruise on his face, which his father couldn't explain because he has trouble waking up, even when a child is screaming in pain and fear in the dark several feet from his sleeping head having fallen out of an adult-sized, unfortified bed... into the corner of a pulled-out dresser drawer (supposedly; according to the grandmother who woke, stretched, and made it downstairs to eventually help my child, alone in the dark, crying until she arrived and his father never woke). Because it is considered such truly incredible luck to be permitted to move children away from their (dysfunctional, diagnosed, documented) father, my lawyer, my kids, and I had to swallow what would be the other conditions of the move. A mother cannot just look into the eyes of a female judge and say, "Look, this guy is no good. He's gone really downhill. He has terrorized me, neglected the kids, and will not be a good influence." Women's words in court get us only so far.

In addition to allowing my abusive ex two weekends each month with the children, he gets thrice weekly video calls, in which he awkwardly tries to converse with them on the limited number of topics that he knows to interest them, asks them questions they can't answer, gives them confusing descriptions of where he is, winds them up, and encourages socially inappropriate behavior like not having to share and screaming as much as they like. I hear my abuser's unstable voice floating through my house three times a week, coaching my children to continue believing in his good cop, wild-and-fun-one status. I tried to tell our legal system that he's a horrible person who had fooled me for too long already, but he gets to loom over the children promoting himself for years to come.

In addition to his daily, weekly, and monthly rights, he gets to have the children for two weeks at a stretch, twice every summer. Twice a summer, the creep that I didn't recognize for too long gets to have my babies for 14 days at a time—without their mommy, their primary caregiver, to comb their hair, make sure they get enough sleep, vegetables that are not baby food purees, sunscreen, baths, learning to share, learning to think of others, or to let them know that not everything has to be a wild tickling match with a weird, wild, unstable energy. We do not live in a system wherein a mother can look at a judge, even a female one, and say, "Look, this is no good. He is not good – not to me, not to his family, not to the only two friends who stick by his unsafe behaviors, not to his co-workers, and not to these children. Let us go. Let me decide how safe my children will be. I will let them know of him, but let me meter it out."

We live in patriarchy, a system that prioritizes a father figure at the expense of a mother figure. I know that my children will benefit from knowing that even a mentally ill or utterly mean father loves them. I understand that all children benefit from knowing much of their history, genetic and otherwise, sooner or later, at some stage of life when knowing things satisfies curious hunger inside of them instead of confusing them and teaching them a lack of boundaries. I accept that they may often prefer their "good cop" who garners their attention as fodder for his ego. But my trauma and their poor education of the heart continue due to the patriarchal system that isn't going to let a mother and children just walk into the sunset while waving, discussing amongst themselves, and occasionally running back for hugs and brief chats. I don't get to testify as to how often and for how long my

11

sweet, innocent, beloved babies should be up close and personal to an evil clown.

My abusive ex gets to continually drip and ooze his patriarchal dysfunction all over my matriarchy, but it's not him alone. My otherwise very thoughtful and competent bosses often don't understand why I am not free to attend extra meetings or trainings at short notice. Why isn't my schedule more flexible? Aren't my children in childcare? Well, no, not officially. You see, I am an adjunct professor. There's a hiring freeze at our public institution, which is constantly being busted on the chops by our state's very masculine governor, who loves going after teachers specifically. So, with only three classes per semester, I make a decent wage for the few hours that I work, but I can't be given more hours and more money, because full time employees cost the public institution benefits (even before Obamacare). So my mother has given up on her income to retire, and on her planned retirement activities, and her beautiful home to provide my children with expert childcare many days per week. This small version of matriarchy continuously saves me from the ever increasing patriarchy of the larger work system that can't fathom why I would like to be paid for more classroom prep, why I can't pop in to a spur-of-the moment meeting, or why I can't grade papers the day after they are turned in.

My superiors, the institution itself, and my students, stuck staunchly in the patriarchal code of our country, cannot even picture what it is to be a single mother: dependent on my personal matriarch for survival, constantly attending to the tiny bodies that depend on me and my mother for everything – missing out on their milestones even as I try to work to support them, and not being supplemented by decent child support because my ex's state formula multiples my hourly income by forty hours a week, pretending that I am full time. I cannot put my children in childcare to attend spontaneous meetings, because an official state child support formula dictates that if a mother has a job, her wage, for support purposes, even paired against a six-figure ex-husband, should be multiplied to paint wildly more income than she actually makes.

It is a good thing that I win in life by having my beautiful children, because it is impossible to win in many other ways. Even with my amazing mother helping me out, I cannot fully escape my abuser, or knowledgeably limit his access to my children. I cannot rise to the professional level expected of me, to move away from needing child support, because I can't afford to put my children in childcare while I work. I cannot end the trauma and after-quakes of trauma due simply to the codified patriarchal values absorbed by our entire legal and political system. My children are the treasures of my life; I wish that I could better protect them. A matriarchy would and does already serve them better than patriarchy ever has.

With Strangers Like These

Kelsey Lueptow

December 12

I sit at the bar after work at the dawn of my third trimester. Sticky oak beneath my elbows. I'm shuffling singles and rotating my dangling ankles. I don't try to join in the cacophony of party stories that echo off to my left where the other waitresses have already cashed out and are sharing an order of calamari. I smile when they ask if they look three months pregnant from eating too much. I lie when they ask if my back hurts, my feet. I smile when they make jokes about vegetarians. Mostly, though, I do not say anything at all. Sticky oak beneath my elbows. Small ovals of plastic pressing the bridge of my nose.

"Who's going to be in the delivery room with you?" my boss, Jane, asks. I've learned in the three months I've worked here that she is anything but subtle, and I start to think that's the thing about strangers or almost-strangers, and usually about bosses.

I say his name—my son's father—and peel down singles to tip out the expo, the bartender, the busser, the hostess, "and my mom, too."

"Do you really want your mom there? In the room with you?" Jane asks while polishing wine glasses with the bartender. A small white rag buffing haloes on stems. "You should really have someone else there. Someone supportive." I cringe.

Jane goes on, "Someone here."

In Victorian times, a wealthy father could abuse and neglect wife and children without losing custody. American coverture was waning, but persistent. Today I carry fistfuls of Shakespeare in my satchel. Blue hard covers and an unfinished essay huff toward my shared apartment. Victorian single mothers were often sent to insane asylums. I don't know how to wear that title yet—scraping, I make a scarlet letter out of red duct tape for Halloween; a nest of hair ties hold my pre-pregnancy jeans up.

At the sticky oak bar, I do not look up from my make believe counting as I cycle through my cash tips over and over again. I don't tell Jane that I've quit expectations cold turkey, and really, I'm not her responsibility.

"What if he doesn't get here in time?" she goes on talking, I go on counting, the smooth wisp of the illuminati pyramid flitting on my fingerpads. "I mean, it's five hours. You should take a Lamaze class, too. He can't be here for that."

"There's one at Mercy," I say. My OB recommends it. She's kind, and sometimes I lie to her questions because her hair is so perfect.

"You should take a Lamaze class with Joy." Jane says this with the emphasis of an imperative.

Cady Stanton and some two thousand supporters protested for equal custodial rights between mothers and fathers in 1869. By the twentieth century, women could have custodial rights in 9 states—with a proper record of morality, purity. No sexual deviance. No deviance. Joy insists that I let her come to Lamaze with me. She insists she has time between three jobs and getting ready for her wedding and law school. She insists there is nothing she would rather do. We are both wearing short-sleeved black tee shirts and dress slacks. The apron covers the gap where my pants cannot clasp. Joy slides her apron coolly across the light oak bar. She takes my number. She will come to Lamaze.

***

December 5

Jane had cornered me in dry storage before the second half of my split shift: "Have you called your mother yet?"

"No, I slept." I shuffled my jacket onto a hook that already had three jackets on it. It slipped off a few times, but I finally got it to stick and turned around.

"Call your mother."

"I will, I just—"

"Call your mother. Today. After work." It was quiet a moment. A couple girls squealed past us. Earlier that morning I dutifully informed Jane that I had received a phone call from the woman who had slept with my boyfriend. Her name was Lily. I said I was doing the best I could. I told her everything was going to be fine.

"Are you OK?"

Everything was going to be fine.

"Yeah."

According to Judith Arcana, the "idealized mother is a woman who is boundlessly giving and endlessly available . . . The idealized father is practically invisible . . . scarcely present, to his son his presence becomes miraculous and precious." Judith was a Jane. She and a secret pack of Chicago women performed over eleven thousand abortions before Roe v. Wade. She was the anti-coat hanger. I could never be a Jane. I'm afraid of getting arrested, that any deviance might remove my son from me. Even when we are only one body. I'm afraid of blood and other people's bodies. But Joy, she could have been a Jane. She worked at Planned Parenthood afternoons she was not at the restaurant. She helped poor, hurting young women. Basically, strangers. She was going to be a lawyer. I could see her, the woman whose slacks always close, whose hair does not frizz, on some stone staircase somewhere walking her crying client to the car. I could see her winning.

There was a flurry of twenty-year-olds in black shirts and jingling champagne flutes overhead as we prepped the back server station. A girl I don't like but don't exactly not-like got an internship with *Cosmo*. That, and she met a boy at a wedding. I didn't have much to add to either discovery and she'd never actually spoken to me before, so I stocked napkins and filled water pitchers. I didn't tell anyone about the phone call. I didn't tell them I had dumped my son's father. I didn't tell them that when Lily called to tell me what he had done to us she was crying—I was not. I just let the secrets settle on my fingers as I mixed a ginger ale.

I did cry on the bus, though. And in the library, and on the walk from the library to the English-Philosophy Building. I did cry after a stranger stood and insisted I take his place at the library computer, and every time the cashiers asked to carry my bags from the Hy-Vee. Sizzling white lights pluming on my shoulder blades. I cried when my mother begged me to come have my baby at home. I cried when I told her, "No," although I aimed it away from the phone. And, I cried when a boy from my Cleopatra acting group shared his rap talents with me—and didn't ask anything about my pregnancy at all.

***

February, March, April

I will not text Joy when it is almost time for Lamaze to start and I am alone. Every other Monday of the next two months, I will sit in a seventies-themed hospital basement and think that she is probably not coming and that's ok. The Berber is burnt orange. The chairs scooped and pale. It's not a big deal. It's not her job. And every other Monday night for the next two months, she will bluster in at two minutes 'til and tell me to breathe when they put up slides about caesarean.

It's estimated that one hundred to one hundred twenty-five thousand children are kidnapped by a non-custodial parent every year. In a study of North American parents from 1960-1981, 0% of women were reported to have "engaged in brainwashing campaigns" of the children, as opposed to 57% of men in the study. 62% of men abused their wives after a split, 37% kindnapped their children, and 67% reported financial motives for seeking custody. The size of the study is too small, but I'm defensive of experiences, stories in sealed rooms. When my son's father comes to Iowa City the week of my due date, I will show him the online child support calculator that estimates he will be ordered to pay $875 a month, based on our income discrepancies. I will say I don't want to go to court and ask for $500 a month. He will laugh and offer to pay $400, no more. We will be sitting on two, squat wooden chairs at a library desktop. It will smell like dust and strangers. I will tell him I do not want to go to court.

When my roommate insists I start timing my contractions and text her, Joy will answer immediately and be over in minutes. I will not want to be a bother, but she will drive us to the hospital anyway in a small, blue car. When they have to give me oxygen, I will tell her I think that the nurses hate me for screaming. Because I can't breathe. For gaining more than the recommended weight. For saying I want a margarita after he is born. She will tell me that's crazy, and I won't tell her that's exactly what I'm afraid of.

When Aliens Knead You

Kelsey Lueptow

THE THINGS THAT YOU HEAR after having a baby are always about looks. So after more than the inherited weight of pregnancy melts away, ribs poking your elbows, you will be called *beautiful!* and *uh-may-zing!* You will smile. You will not say that your depletion was due to bare cupboards save the WIC supplements. When asked how you lost "the weight," like it's an uninvited houseguest or an infestation, you will say yoga instead of describing what it feels like waiting on student loans and child support, ignoring your hunger while scrubbing the abandonment issues off your shoelaces. Never mind that your face is pale and your fingers shake and you get dizzy—a lot. Never mind.

In line at the DMV is the first place you do not recognize yourself. Borrowed jeans the only thing that will stay up. A little fuzz behind your eyelids, you're not sure if this is what you really look like or not. Needle straight thighs. Straight lines. The four walls of a new ID for a new job (where the secretary tells you that you do not look like you just had a baby) frame your face. Frame your angles. You take your glasses off for the glare. You look *beautiful.* At Mother's Day brunch with your family the waiter is an elementary school classmate who says he did not recognize you and you are meant to take this as a compliment. Amid all the ways you are hurting, the truth is you take this as a compliment. You hold it in your cheeks while adjusting your son's fedora. While saying thank you. While trying not to look like you haven't eaten in weeks in front of your parents. They might worry. You look beautiful. You fix his fedora.

At the grocery store for the first time in six weeks, you read your oversized WIC vouchers like scripture. For June 2011:

VOID IF ALTERED – VOID IF VENDOR DOES NOT HAVE A VALID OWA WIC CONTRACT
ONLY WIC APPROVED FOODS MAY BE PURCHASED – NO SUBSTITUTIONS ALLOWED

97-97   Family ID: 372XXX   Name: Kelsey N. Lueptow

4 Can(s) 14-16 oz. Beans, Refried or Black
2 Gallons of Milk – Unflavored Only
The Humiliating Eye Rolls from 16 Year Old Bag Boys
1 Lbs. Vegetables, Frozen and/or Fresh
The Flush From Somewhere Below Your Neck, Below The Dip Of The Baby Carrier Into The Cart, Below Your Fingernails, Behind Your Eye Sockets, Beneath The Grinding Of Your Organs In Protest. No Substitutions.
3 Can(s) 10-12 oz. Juice (Frozen), Approved Brands
36 oz. Cereal or Less, Approved Brands
9 Can(s) Formula, Similac Sensitive

It takes you over an hour to assemble the cart. You aim for accuracy, for a small line with a kind smile. You have trouble reading people these days. You have trouble reading. Your first trip to a bar postpartum, your son will be a howling silence during his father's weekend—something you are pretending you can cope with. And strange women will approach you and lift their shirts and tell you that you are *so lucky* you don't look like this. You are *so lucky* you don't have stretch marks, like an alien kneaded your stomach gently when you were most malleable, a metaphysical massage with surreal implications. Co-workers will ask you behind the restaurant between their Marlboro green puffs to lift your shirt. And you will oblige them, the women, the co-waitresses, and they will say: *huh.*

The Joys of Single Motherhood

Jennifer Kimmel

MY EXPERIENCE AS A SINGLE MOTHER has been a wonderful, healing and powerful gift. My family's life is now filled with unbridled joy, love, healing, creativity, freedom and an easy harmony that is all our own. A man does not dictate the mood, the tone, or the rules in this house. It is our home, run by a strong, grounded woman and her children, filled with healthy, singing souls unsquelched. It is a workable democracy cushioned from, not crushed by, the patriarchy.

I suspect there are quite a few similar stories out there. Women and their children, breathing happy sighs of relief, moving about unburdened by the demands of a domineering male presence, discovering the sweet taste of freedom. It is because, not in spite of my status as a single mother that my family's life is so genuinely peaceful, happy and authentic, so much more are our own, and so much more about what we deserve and not what the patriarchy demands.

Opening a piece about single motherhood by stating my family's happiness derives specifically from what is often referred to as a "broken home," will certainly open me to judgment. To be honest, I don't give a fiddler's fart who our truth offends. I am well beyond the point of apologizing to anyone, but I am quite willing to share my thoughts in the hope they might resonate and perhaps be helpful.

I remember commiserating with other single moms on a chat site who were also struggling under huge financial burdens, and we were accused by someone afflicted with simple-minded pettiness of playing the "single mothers card." At first, I was intensely annoyed to hear yet another serious social issue flippantly reduced to something as trivial as a playing card. Then, being a bit whimsical by nature, I thought it would be better to turn the idea on its head. Why not pull together as women, rather than judging as this woman had?

Each single mom in a group would be entitled to a deck. One card could be a free nap, another a leisurely bath, one a pee without an audience. There might be a card for one's laundry basket to help manage the never-ending pile, a milk and bread until next payday card, a sleepless night rejuvenation card, a someone else makes dinner card, a card that morphs into a lovely bottle of wine, a shoulder to cry on card. By sticking together, we could provide each other the support needed to enable us to more fully enjoy our lives with our children.

Single motherhood is not a game, nor is it a joke. It is far from easy but it can be glorious in its own right. The rest of the magical deck could easily be filled with delightful, intimate moments with our children, unencumbered by the awkward negotiations of co-parenting within the patriarchy, a task I was unable to accomplish and no longer feel guilty about but, rather, choose to celebrate.

Even as at least half of us are raising kids essentially on our own, there is still society's insistence that shame be brought upon single mothers. We screwed up, we opened our legs, we disobeyed, we made rash decisions, we expected something more for ourselves than our mothers and got too big for our britches. The stigma the patriarchy insists on attaching to us stems from nothing more than the malicious intent of coercing us into submission. It is obvious when we look at the huge financial strain under which most of us are forced to live. We single moms are to be penitent martyrs, gratefully accepting what little is thrown our way. As supposedly fallen women, we are supposed to be deferential, asexual and saint-like. We somehow did not sacrifice enough of ourselves to earn the proper family unit. We failed to sufficiently enable the man to do his part, whatever part he saw fit to play while we picked up the pieces.

We are expected to keep the fathers of our children around, no matter the cost to us and our children. The burden of maintaining a bond between father and child often lies with us. As always, it is somehow our fault when men fail us and our children.

Let me share a bit of my own story at this point. I don't think it is particularly rare or unique. I grew up poor and neglected in an emotionally abusive home. My mother treated my siblings and I like burdensome interlopers. My father was a raving racist, misogynist, paranoid Napoleon and my mother worshiped at his feet. The needs of her children were seen as an annoyance, serving only to distract her from her desire to please him.
I have never quite figured out what made my mother tick, but I suspect it was, in a part, a need to be loved and accepted within the patriarchal system that wounded and oppressed her. What I will never understand is her unwillingness to love and protect her children from that very same beast.

My childhood was riddled with sexual abuse. When as a little girl, I was found masturbating, and I was punished and told I made Jesus cry. At age five, it was discovered I was being molested by an older sadistic male cousin. It is I who was shamed. When it became undeniably clear I was being sexually abused by a male teacher, no help or retribution was offered, just an interrogation about what I had done to provoke the situation. I was ten years old.

I internalized this inscrutable blame I received as a shameful part of the inconvenience of my existence. I did not understand what I did to provoke these assaults. I was especially confused as I had developed strong, natural sexual feelings when very young and was convinced, as I am sure many other girls were, that I was a dirty, worthless, deeply flawed creature.

It is estimated that at least one in five women experienced some form of sexual abuse as a child. What harm this does us, we can only begin to address when given the space, support and peace we need to heal. Reclaiming yourself can take a lifetime.

I suffered a massive, crippling depression at the age of twelve. I rarely thought of much but death and dying for months. When I tried in resigned desperation to reach out, I was told I was selfish, imagining things and a drama queen.

By the time I was an early teen I had lost my voice, my instinct, any semblance of self-esteem, and all but the basic ability to protect myself from psychological and other abuses. I wandered about in a daze, bumping into things, tripping over my own feet. I was constantly covered in bruises I could not remember acquiring. I was determined to blend into walls. I put effort into nothing but getting from day to day without harm. When I absolutely had to speak, I apologized compulsively to everyone. I was sorry for daring take up space on the planet.

While perhaps extreme, I don't think the feelings I suffered as a girl and young woman are rare within a patriarchal society. I did eventually begin to realize that my experience was due to forces outside of myself, and I wanted to heal. I knew what would be most helpful to me was to create my own family and love and protect my children as I wanted to be loved and protected.

This was a reasonable plan in theory but to find a suitable partner when you are the walking wounded in a sea of patriarchal sexism, abuse, hate, violence, and objectification is close to impossible.

This leads me to the point that, so often, single moms are chastised for not choosing better, not valuing ourselves enough to withhold our natural sexual instincts and for procreating with the "wrong kind" of man. From what planet do these sanctimonious beraters come? What exactly do they see in the world around them? The place is hardly swimming with well-adjusted, enlightened, forward-thinking, feminist men. I am afraid it is quite the opposite.

Most of the time, young women settle. To one degree or another, we decide to adapt ourselves, as we have been groomed to do, rather than attempt the daunting task of challenging society and instead we settle. I know I did.

How many women when at the age for choosing a mate for the purposes of creating a family are fully or even partially aware of their own psychology? How many of us realize the extent to which the patriarchy has stifled, dismissed, objectified and abused us and the pool of men and women from which we must choose? How deeply does this affect the decisions we make? Decisions for which, the vast majority of the time, women only are held accountable.

How people go about choosing a life partner after growing up in our society is far more complicated a process than the patriarchy would have us believe.

I met a man I thought was suitably different if little else. He was born abroad, I was eager to leave my childhood home behind and eventually we and our children returned to his country. But the magical transformation I expected from this journey, even after years of ruthless domination, neglect and harmful, selfish behavior - something I attributed to depression after countless nights listening to him cry with homesickness - instead became a further nightmare. I had seen the warning signs before this crisis point, but I ignored them thinking I deserved no better. I had been told as much, my entire life.

My husband spiraled further into depression, and the relationship became undeniably abusive. He barely allowed me or the children to leave the house, let alone helped us integrate into our new country. We spent an entire year cooped up without heat or hot water with a disturbingly depressed and remorselessly apathetic man. I was 3000 miles away from all I knew at the whim of a very sick, very selfish person.

I knew I had to get myself and my children out and I did. It was incredibly daunting but with the help of other women who noticed and acknowledged my plight, I did it. And while doing so, I finally came into myself. I realized my incredible strength as I protected my children. I realized my worth as I was cherished by new and loving friends. I regained my voice in my constant protest against the unacceptable. I was no longer ashamed of or confused by my sexuality but reveled in a lover who did not tread upon me and respected me for all that I was.

In choosing to leave my husband and create a life for my children and I as a single parent, I found the healing I had yearned for most of my life and was able to nurture and guide my beloved children from a place of confidence and strength.

We are all, women and men, shaped and damaged by the patriarchy. We are all in the process of healing from its relentless savagery, while also struggling to live within it. While I do not blame men alone for society's sad predicament, I am no longer willing to enable male complicity. Whether a man claims to be innocent or beligerently embraces their part in perpetuating violence and abuse, the results are the same, just with varying degrees of devastation.

I am weary of combatting the twisted indoctrination both men and women cling to obtusely, so fearful are they of change. I am tired of constantly having to box my corner, shield my children, struggle for the basic acknowledgment of my rights as a human being.

I realize some couples find ways to live traditionally under the umbrella of the patriarchy. I could not and will no longer try. It is too dangerous for the likes of me. I may still bend. I may still capitulate. I might accept the unacceptable. I might rationalize abuse as something I deserve. I might finally drown trying to navigate the treacherous waters of the system that oppresses us all and finally lose myself for good.

Everyone, especially women, knows that a certain willingness to accommodate others for the sake of an easy flow in your day or week or life is necessary. But many women like me, after suffering years of abuse under the patriarchy, struggle to know and maintain our boundaries, or to recognize what is a reasonable compromise and what is bullying, malicious dominance or flat-out abuse.

I have only just found shelter for my once barely flickering flame, have only just scraped enough of myself back together to thrive and be the mother I want to be for my children. I will not jeopardize this paradise I have created for us trying to fit into any so-called normal, patriarchically acceptable existence.

My time with my children is precious, as is the life we have reclaimed and are now living as we see fit. A life we shape and choose every day, having struggled to step outside the suffocating box of male domination. We are doing it our way, patriarchy be damned.

The recovery necessary from a life rife with misfortune due to misogyny is why I am unapologetically joyous about the opportunity to raise my three gorgeous children alone, without domination, without deference disguised as compromise, without patriarchally-imposed emotional injury to any of us. Our home is a haven of chaotic bliss, full of love, healing and adventure. We have our own unique way of living and no one gets in our way.

I doubt I would have escaped our abusive situation without the warm circle of women who held me and my children tight throughout our struggle. This sisterhood gently guided us to the other side. We are strong now. We have our life back. We have triumphed. The supernatural strength that comes from women pulling together can do far more than transform the lives of individual women. We can transform the planet. That is why the patriarchy is so very afraid of us. That is why such an enormous amount of energy and resources are spent trying to divide and squelch us. I'll comply no more. No more silencing single mothers, no more poverty and abuse for our beloved children. It is time, my sisters. Let our collective goddess shift the earth, let our fierce strength, love, and joy be unleashed, let the planet be healed.

£4 Billion

Louise Pennington

£4 billion.

This is the outstanding arrears of child maintenance owed in England and Wales. According to a report by the charity Gingerbread called *Missing Maintenance*, the Department of Works and Pensions (DWP) estimates that only £467 million will ever be recovered.[9] This leaves nearly one half of single parent families, the vast majority headed by women, living in poverty.

The current Conservative government is in the process of closing the Child Support Agency (CSA) to replace it with the Child Maintenance Service, which charges women £20 for the privilege of opening a file and then a sum each month if some semblance of the maintenance is actually paid.[10] The new vaunted system has seen only 53% of the families registered receiving maintenance with 90 000 people having not paid during one three-month period. There is already nearly £53 million in unpaid maintenance. Many of the families will receive only negligible amounts of money, as the DWP does not require the full maintenance to be paid in order for the account to be registered as compliant. Realistically, a father of 4 earning £70 000 a year can pay only £5 a month and still be included within the 53% statistic.[11]

---

9 Report: *Missing Maintenance*. Gingerbread: Single Parents, Equal Families. (June 2016). PDF: http://www.gingerbread.org.uk/uploads/media/17/9809.pdf
10 'Use the Child Maintenance Service or Child Support Agency'. https://www.gov.uk/child-maintenance/overview. Accessed 29.8.16.
11 'How we work out child maintenance: a step by step guide." Child Maintenance Service.
(https://www.gov.uk/government/uploads/system/uploads/attachment_data/file/325219/how-we-work-out-child-maintenance.pdf) Accessed 29.8.16.

Equally problematic is the fact that the Child Maintenances Service is actively writing to the primary caregivers to request they 'forgive' the debt owed by non-paying fathers[12] - as though the primary caregivers of children, who are overwhelmingly women, can neglect to pay rent, council tax and the credit card debts they rack up buying groceries knowing these debts will be 'forgiven'. As Polly Toynbee makes clear,

> Some 90% of CSA cases have now been transferred over to the CMS, but only 13% of mothers affected have decided to pay the new fees and apply to the CMS: the DWP must be pleased, as it had publicly estimated that 63% would pursue their claims. All the pressure in official letters is to deter mothers. The £20 fee may be a mild block, along with charging fathers 4%, but the evidence suggests mothers just give up when prodded by these letters.[13]

Charging mothers to use the Child Maintenance Service is simply a way for the government to abdicate responsibility. They are very clear that the sole purpose is to force more parents into dealing with child maintenance themselves. In doing so, they have refused to recognise the reason why men, and it is overwhelmingly men, refuse to pay maintenance: it is both a punishment and a form of control over their former partners. This is male entitlement writ large by men who do not care about the welfare of their children.

We need to start calling the refusal to pay maintenance what it really is: financial child abuse. Forcing your children to live in poverty because you cannot be bothered to support them or

---

12 Polly Toynbee. 'Why the silence on the scandal of unpaid child maintenance?'. *Guardian*. (16.5.2016).
13 Polly Toynbee. 'Why the silence on the scandal of unpaid child maintenance?'. *Guardian*. (16.5.2016).

refusing to punish the mother are not the signs of 'good fathers.' It is the hallmark of an abusive father.

It is not difficult to implement child maintenance policies that are effective and ensure that men cannot hide their assets. Placing the Child Maintenance Service under the heading of HM Revenue & Customs so that child maintenance is garnished directly from the salary of the non-resident parent. This coupled with actual punitive policies for those who refuse to pay, such as a fee for every missed payment, interest accrued on outstanding payments, and the use of enforcement agents (bailiffs) to confiscate personal property, and, potentially, criminal proceedings would see an immediate increase in the number of men who start to pay their maintenance.[14]

There is a quote bandied about in discussions of child contact and child maintenance that says 'children aren't pay per view', as though children were nothing more than a possession to be passed about. As with Women's Aid campaign, *Safe Contact Saves Lives*, we need to stop talking about children as possessions and start talking about children's rights.[15] Children have the right to live free from violence. Children also have the right to live outwith poverty.

The erasure of men's financial responsibility for their children, supported by government policy, is an absolute disgrace. It is, simply, state-sanctioned child abuse.

---

14 Canada also includes the suspension of drivers licenses and passports as part of their maintenance enforcement programs. http://www.justice.gc.ca/eng/fl-df/enforce-execution/pwo-pqp.html. Accessed 29.8.2016.

15 'Child First: Safe Contact Saves Lives'. Women's Aid England/ Wales. https://www.womensaid.org.uk/childfirst/ Accessed 29.8.16

The Pulse

Lucía Martínez

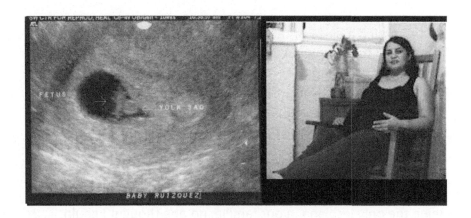

ESTRELLA de ORO

Jessica Ruizquez

MY SWEET LOVE, it was on Thanksgiving Day at Nani's house that I began to pray for you.

My prima tied a piece of thread to a needle and held it over the palms of all the women in our familia. The needle swung in a circle for each girl child and back and forth for each boy child-the mujer had or would have. The needle swung with painful accuracy telling of each miscarriage and abortion our mujeres had known. I watched in amazement as the needle told things my prima didn't know.

When it was my turn, the women of our familia casually watched. Being the only lesbiana in our familia, no one thought I could possibly want or have a child. When my prima held the needle over my palm, it stood completely still. My heart filled with sadness. I asked her to do it again, and again. Each time it did not move. My prima said you could always adopt. My heart cried.

I had always wanted children but did not want to give birth. I thought it would be my mujer that would birth our children. Watching the needle stand in complete stillness, my soul cried for you. I cried for you. My body would never know you. I would never know how you felt growing inside of me. I would never know the beautiful milagro of creation, a baby growing inside of me- birth. I would never know you, my sweet love.

That night my cuerpo cried for you, I cried until my tears turned into prayers. I prayed to the Virgen, Tonantzine, asking our Madre to make me a Mama, your Mama. I lived in quietness for the next few months, praying for you, calling you, dreaming of you, you my sweet love...I prayed for you.

Your Mama is a strong two-spirited mujer, a proud ESTRELLA de ORO lesbiana. For me there was no other choice but artificial insemination to get pregnant. Living in Phoenix, I had many fertility doctors to choose from. I chose the leading fertility specialist in Arizona, an arrogant white man who wore all black and spoke of fertility and of "getting me pregnant" as if he were the Creator herself. We began the fertility process; he with his drugs, ultrasounds and follicle measurements; me with my altar, prayers, fertility circles, fertility foods and bendiciones from women elders. I was calling you, my sweet love.

Soon after I began the fertility process, I moved to El Paso. Living on the Frontera came with so many beautiful regalos. I was living on the tierra of our people. For the first time in my brown vida, I was part of the majority. I was excited with sueños of being a Mama in this land, growing a brown baby in a brown community. You, my sweet love would know your history, your cultura, your people, your tradiciones, and your ancestors.

Feeling you so close, my sweet love, I quickly began my search for a fertility doctor here in El Paso. I found there was only one, but he was Mexicano! In Phoenix I never had the option of a person of color and now the doctor assisting me was my own gente! Making my first appointment, I was asked many questions: "what is your medical condition and why are you having difficulties getting pregnant?" I explained I do not have any fertility problems. I am simply and proudly an ESTRELLA de ORO. I am a gold star lesbian, I have never been with a man and in this most sacred gift of conception, I would make no exception.

Very quickly and carefully I was told that the doctor, my brown brother, would not accept patients like me, lesbianas. I soon found there were no other fertility doctors in El Paso. The closest doctor was 6 hours away. I decided to go back to the arrogant white man in Phoenix, whose response to me being lesbiana was "I can get anyone pregnant." So every other month, I went to Phoenix for treatment. I would stay there for the two days of the initial cycle of fertility drugs and monitoring and then drive back to El Paso. After about a week and half, it would be time for insemination, and then I would drive back to Phoenix. I did this a few times and did not get pregnant. My suegra said "of course you are not getting pregnant; after a woman makes love, she lies around in bed relaxing, sleeping; it is when the body is still, calm and full of love that is when the baby comes."

I was driving back to El Paso in a rental car, hurrying to get back to work. My employers in the Women's Studies Program were understanding about my beautiful struggle but were also inconvenienced by all of the time I spent traveling. To this day, I am grateful for their patience and support.

The arrogant doctor was outraged that I was being denied treatment and had to travel back and forth to Phoenix two times for each insemination. He called and wrote a formal letter to the doctor in El Paso, asking him to accept me as a patient. The El Paso doctor said he would treat me conditionally. He said he was doing this as a favor for the Phoenix doctor. The El Paso doctor agreed to monitor my follicle growth, which were the daily vaginal ultrasounds, and administer the hormone injections but refused to do the insemination. After I was given the hormone injection that would cause my eggs to drop, I had 36 hours to get to Phoenix for insemination. I would not let myself feel discouraged, overwhelmed or angered by this violent homophobia. I was already your Mama, your strong, determined, revolutionary

Mama. I was in the movement of creation, of life, of being a Mama, your Mama. I would not allow the bad energy that comes with homophobia enter our sacred space. I met that energy with a peaceful resistance of prayer and compassion. You, my sweet love, my greatest teacher, were already teaching me, showing me a new fight, a revolution through the unconditional love of a Mama.

After many unsuccessful tries, the El Paso doctor agreed to also do the inseminations. Making sure that I understood his position and his view of my place. He told me "you got in through the back door." I would not let his negativity and homophobia enter my beautiful sacred space of creation. I thought of him as one of the many prayers, intentions, songs, sueños, foods, baños, and tears of creation that I gave and accepted to call you- to bring you to me, my sweet love.

Now, I would no longer have to travel to Phoenix. I could do the entire process here in El Paso. Looking out the window of our small apartment on the Frontera, I would concentrate on the massive Mexican flag swaying in the wind- the wind that freely crosses borders. Dreaming of you growing in the space of Nepantla, the space in-between borders, I prepared my body to receive the morning fertility injections in my stomach. The injections began the monthly treatment that I came to know as my honor of being your proud ESTRELLA de ORO Mama. When I went to doctor appointments, I took the Peruvian fabric given to me as a fertility gift and placed it over the paper on the exam table. This fabric of intention and love is what I laid on while I was inseminated. I then went home and spent the day in bed, my bed, being loved up, while my body welcomed the life force that is you.

After a year and a half, on the seventh insemination, I became pregnant with you, my sweet love. I was inseminated and conceived you on Thanksgiving Day. I think back to the Thanksgiving Day at Nanis, when the needle stood still over my palm. My tears of sadness turned into tears of prayer and are now tears of an indescribable love. You have given me a new true meaning to Thanksgiving Day. You, my sweet love has healed many old historical wounds and have helped me to meet homophobia with a fight of peaceful resistance and have redefined this day of giving thanks. Tlazocamati Madre Tonantzin, Tlazocamati Virgen, Tlazocamati Paz.

Married to Patriarchy

Solana Simpson

PATRIARCHY EXISTS TO SERVE THE INTERESTS OF MEN, and in our country, most notably white men. Our laws were made by men, and our family court structure was made by men. The whole structure exists, on the whole, to benefit the patriarchy's interests. My journey into that started in a different system of patriarchy – my marriage.

At the beginning of my marriage's unraveling, my ex-husband gave me a list. His list included the requirements for my staying married to him. On the list were dictates that included: begin every sentence with an "I" statement; agree with 100% of what he says; agree with 100% of his parenting decisions; he has to be in charge of where my things go; that I must cease to have strong feelings; that I spend what he tells me to spend on groceries; that I inform him when my menstrual cycle is happening; that I believe everything he says; and that my Facebook and emails are always open to him. When I asked him what the point of this list was, he replied, "Control. I need control." I was one broken person then, and also scared of what he would do, so I told him I would give him his list. That wasn't good enough, as he told me – and so we were soon divorced.

As part of our divorce process, we were required to mediate. At the first mediation, I was greeted by a stack of motions detailing my depression and inadequacy as a mother. My ex agreed to provide child support. Allowing myself to be bullied, I agreed to his parenting plan, which was no reflection of what kind of parent he actually was at that time. It meant I had significantly less time with my children, but I wanted to avoid going to court at all costs

41

and knew that the court system favors 50/50 parenting plans, even for small children, and mine was close enough to not be 50/50 that I didn't want to rock the boat.

We had a second mediation on property and financial issues. By then I had mustered up some courage and was not as agreeable. We were headed to trial.

Right after that, my ex switched attorneys and filed a motion to discontinue child support based on the judge not signing the agreement right away. This was six months after he agreed to pay child support in the amount he offered and according to the chart. That was the moment at the top of the roller coaster's first big hill, only there was no sense of play and fun and an end at four minutes. This was a descent into a place that seemed to make absolutely no sense to me, where everything was upside down, and no one cared about my ex's character. That place was family court.

I should back up here and provide more information. My ex is someone you might see walking down the street. He is a holistic bodyworker and appears to be a pretty interesting, cool person. His family is close. One of them is a psychotherapist, one a deacon in the Catholic church, and another one is an experienced social worker. My ex's father was a prominent divorce attorney in our town. My ex grew up hearing things like, "logic would dictate..." as a critical way to address his behavior. He was, in the most important ways, brought up in a home court of law. There is a sickness that permeates his family, and they all agree to participate in it. As a result, his family is one of the most enmeshed families I have ever seen. I often compare them to the "Borg" from Star Trek. If you insult one by non-compliance, you've insulted them all. If you are on one's blacklist, you are also on everyone else's. There is no grace and certainly no middle ground. And there is no one else that matters outside of the family.

His mother also has money. Because of their resources, anything their son wants or needs, he gets. He was never taught how to be a contributing adult, nor that he is capable of supporting himself fully. Years after our divorce, I had a bizarre, heated conversation with his mother, where she repeated my words back to me in a mocking way, and proclaimed her endless love for her son and said that she would give him all the money he needs to take me to court. Not to pay for lessons for the children. Not to pay for their tuition. Not to enrich their lives in any way. But to fund a war against their mother.

After our trial regarding child support issues, my ex decided to stop paying child support. For the next year and a half, he refused to pay child support. In the meantime, the motions kept coming. I remember there were four months once where I did not receive a motion. Eight months after our trial, the judge handed down a verdict. He had to pay child support. More motions and appeals followed.

In the meantime, parenting with him was a nightmare. One time, I was visiting my old neighbor, who lived next door to my ex. I didn't know the kids were home, but as I was readying to leave they spotted me from their upstairs window. My little boy, who was barely four at the time, started to run down the stairs to hug me before I left. The next thing I heard were his cries from inside the house as his father prevented him from coming out to see me. My ex is the slippery kind, for his parenting of the children is not overtly abusive. And my constant fear is that my children will normalize some of his more bizarre behaviors. I have two children from my first marriage, and he was incredibly harsh with them. He

43

did not allow them to pursue their interests without his input and control, and he insisted that they do things they were not comfortable doing. That is another story and I did not protect my daughters as I should have. They do not speak to him or his family to this day, even though they had spent nearly ten years of family togetherness through dinners, birthdays, and holidays.

My ex's parenting skills are still relatively non-existent. He recently went on vacation with the children and my youngest sustained what he thought was a concussion. He had my son call me to tell me that he hit his head, then got on the phone to tell me he thought my son had a concussion. I prompted him to take my son to the hospital and he did. But he would not give me the name of the town, only the name of the hospital. I was not even clear what state they were in. He refused to give me that information and when I asked to speak to the doctor, he said, "You don't need to know that." He did not tell me my son was throwing up and did not give me clear information – then he stood between me and the doctor.

Even worse, he answers emails less than half of the time, refuses to make schedule switches, and puts me in positions where I am "damned if I do, damned if I don't."

When we filed to hold him in contempt for not paying child support, he kept very properly and quite legally disagreeing with the court about his obligation. I knew the system was messed up when at his contempt hearing, right after he had handed me a check for nearly 18 months of back child support, the judge congratulated us for "working it out." The judge, right there, supported his nonsense, and made me realize what a complete joke family court is. That judge retired shortly after this and a new judge was voted in to take his place.

Four months after she was voted in, the court of appeals ruled on his child support appeal, and so another body of judges told him he was obligated to pay child support. The next month, he filed to find me in contempt for various minor schedule infractions, mostly involving my engaging in tit-for-tat as a way to stop him from manipulating the schedule. For example, he would make flight arrangements on a long weekend and schedule to return four or five hours past his scheduled time. But he would not ask me for this adjustment, and he would tell me the day before, despite my requests that he simply communicate with me about the schedule. He refused. He also filed to terminate child support. The new judge agreed with him completely and terminated his child support, as well as finding me in contempt and ordering me to pay is attorney's fees to the tune of $2300.

Now I am not receiving child support. I have grappled with the realization that I have no partner in raising my children, that I never really did. He refuses to contribute to the children's school tuition or supply fees, and is now deliberately working less to show the court how poor he is. Yet he somehow manages, with the unfaltering aid of his mother, to keep those expensive motions coming. In fact, I have something worse than having no co-parent at all. I have a hindrance, someone who seeks to financially ruin me and someone who uses a willing system to carry out his manipulation and control. This is essential patriarchy, the collusion of an individual's power-over dominance with an abusive system already in place to support his superiority.

I am now in college full time. I do not have my degree, despite the fact that I am in my late 40's. I work full time as a teacher. I take on extra jobs as an artist and a musician. And that doesn't include the time I spend parenting my children – or dealing with the constant drama that has become this court case. I take on odd jobs for sewing, singing lessons, and artwork commissions. My plate is too full. If I can work my ass off to support my kids, why the hell is he spending his time memorizing statutes in an attempt to retaliate against me? Does he really think this somehow supports his children?

That is what is most disappointing for me, that none of this seems to take into account the children. I have to come to grips with my deep disappointment in their father as a person. A father who is present and loving to his children and does not seek to break their mother emotionally, financially, or otherwise. A real father knows that, regardless of how much he hates their mother, his children benefit when he meets his obligations. My ex could never be put upon to model respect, kindness, and support for his own children's mother, and neither could his family. It's a sad double whammy.

He is not a father. He is, in every way, a stubborn, foolish dictator. One of the hardest things to deal with has been the status of my situation. Meaning, I am somewhere in between severe domestic violence and "normal." My ex once pushed me down during our marriage, so hard it broke my thumb, but there was never the ongoing cycle of violence with the typical honeymoon phase and build up to a repeat.

I could never show the bruises where he hit me repeatedly, because it didn't happen. I could never insist that he screamed names and profanities at me constantly, because his tactic was using stony silence to demonstrate how I suddenly didn't exist during a conflict. There was, however, the low-level poisonous contempt for me that permeated our whole marriage.

This was one thing I could always count on: that my husband deemed me beneath him, incapable of producing a valid thought, irrational because I had feelings, and merely an object there to serve his whims. And the implication was that his thoughts, his wishes, his desires were always superior in every way to mine, and were the only thoughts that counted.

But this kind of abuse is not enough in a family court system where, if an abused mother brings to light that she is abused, it doesn't matter to a system that Solomon-style, takes the children and splits them between loving mother and documented abuser. If this is the status, how on earth would the court system discredit a controlling, manipulative man? They don't care. *That man* has the same rights to his children as I do. It doesn't matter what he models for the children, or that he doesn't support them. At that point, it isn't a mother's rights or father's rights issue, it is a children's rights issue. If our culture cannot even see their way through the inherent injustice of an unsafe, overtly violent situation, how is it going to serve families like mine – where the abuse is covert and pernicious, and where my ex uses the court system itself to punish and subjugate me?

My answer to that is the system is not set up to serve families and children at all. It is set up to serve the very people who created it: white men. It is set up to receive all of their projection, inherent role dominance, and the desires of men. I was married to patriarchy, and I am still fighting it every day.

The End of What Never Was

Nicola O'Hanlon

I'm done with looking for answers,
and staring at your face for signs
that I just might be valuable.
Starving for some glimmer of hope,
convinced I see one I'd run with it for days
greedily devouring it to keep me
high enough to support my
happy ever after dream,
but that dream was
always less than I deserve.
There's never enough time or money
or opportunity to love me Is there?
Always a million fucking miles away
in another poxy galaxy
where I'm the alien, the strange one
the circus entertainment afforded worthless platitudes
or beaten down and isolated by hate.
But there's always words,
coming from every corner of our minds,
only you can't survive on them for long.
We all string words together
like pretty delicate daisy chains
so they appear to mean something beautiful.
Now your pretty isn't pretty to me anymore
no fake bullshit nonsense whipped up
to keep you happy.
Fuck you and your expectations of me.

All the shit you screamed and screamed into
my open mind emptied itself out somewhere.
I'm not turning myself inside out for you anymore
nor waiting for your "that's acceptable" nod of the head.
I'm not listening to your warnings of danger
nor threats to leave,
you know where the door is.
Now you fear what you tried to suppress,
The WOMAN, the ESSENCE of THE DIVINE.
I survive, The WARRIOR QUEEN of my own life.
I pour my children into this world
to cleanse the filth with which you ruled.
It is their beauty and brilliance
Which you cannot fathom.
Well look closely my love.
THEY COME FROM ME.

Mother and Child

Arna Baartz

Little Ballerinas

Colleen Joy Miller

THERE YOU WERE. Your tiny hands clearly formed, laying on the porcelain. Red rims arranged around you—like a somber, suburban jellyfish.

There he was. A giant, wealthy, orange gas light with a swinging mallet that hung low and hateful between narcissistic legs. There I was begging on my knees for his help while he scowled in disgust at the desperation he creates in me.

There I was, up the mimosa tree that sheltered me from the insanity. Her branches held me with kind passivity when no other could. The same tree that he chain-sawed to the stump two weeks after I left for college.

I couldn't carry the weight of all their hopes and dreams and you, my darling, couldn't even be carried to term.

My heart holds an expansive ridge-visions of what you might have grown to become under my crooked and colorful shadow... and the visions are equally magnificent and terrifying.

And perhaps, like the mimosa frond that has a singular, final, ending-place, it is where and what I am supposed to be.

I think it is enough, right now, that I grow my own branches off this sturdy trunk, give thanks to the root system I fought like hell to nurture as I came to fruition in the shadow of giggling Tickle Deodorant ads and slut shaming.

Here I am. My loving tree inside me now and my one year old darling fast asleep.

Marital Status

Susannah Gregan

, i am married
to the Government
He is the breadwinner
i missed out on
in my virginal years.
He is a polygamist
we are His whores
and His bastards.
nonetheless
we are grateful
for His kindness
as we mostly do not
have ancestral lands
to return to
where
weather permitting
toil persisting
sustenance awaits

For My Daughter Who Now Walks Before Me

Louise M. Hewett

IT IS LATE. I have just finished writing for the evening although my mind is still restless and full of questions. I am always full of questions and feelings, and dreams.

> 'In the night I dreamed. It was my wedding day and I wore a white gown, but as I walked into the ceremonial field the light changed and a threshold darkness seemed to collect at the edges of vision. It reminded me of the sky in a dream I'd had some months ago, a dream of the Antlered One that had come to tell me that my life was about to change. Yes, and many things had changed since that dream had shaken through my soul. Where was the Antlered One, now, where was the One, in me? For if I understood anything about wedding symbolism it was that there was union, that the parts knew and understood themselves to be as one. In that dream the Antlered One had transformed into a shape for such union, and the deep sense of being totally known, totally naked, and totally supported had carried me through and into a new life, a new being.'

I wrote this for the novel I'm currently working on, but I dreamed it a few nights ago, finding answers to my questions in those strange fields of vision. This morning I wake thinking of my day. What new life? What new being? Art History & Theory homework awaits, which interests me but is the new necessity I must do in order to be paid an income. I remind myself how fortunate I am to be studying Art History, to have bed, house, food, car, shoes. I am a single mother. Two of my four children are young, nine and twelve, and one is on the Autism Spectrum. There are issues. The three of us are all seeing a psychologist and I am, at the moment, just able to financially prioritise this for two of us. My autistic son's support is currently from the government.

I get up, I begin. Everything is slow. I am slow, worn out, struggling with depression, and frustrated with myself. I shower, I prepare my medication to prevent further stroke. The necessity of slow action makes me think of my grandmother, who was very slow, and very sensitive, like me. I think of her outwardly simple life, her long passionless marriage, of our conversations about her life and the dream I have of writing a book about my female ancestors. I remember that my grandmother had a nervous breakdown at the age of 21. I remember that my great grandmother was a single mother with nine children, and in a far worse economic situation than I.

I am a single mother and I am very fortunate. I am educated and educate myself. I have time to think and reflect. To write stories. I am paid a basic income dependent on the fact that I fulfill requirements, although none of these requirements involve caring for my children. I must either look for and find a job, or study at least 15 hours a week. I am studying for a Bachelor of Visual Art, and must fulfill 18 hours a week. It is overwhelming for me. I must visit the employment agency. I am on the wrong stream. I have fatigue. Paper work must be provided on the correct days or there are consequences. On my low income I must provide housing and pay for everything required to function in the society in which I live, for my children to attend school and also function in society. I also receive regular financial support from the father of my children, so I am very fortunate indeed.

I do not need to prostitute myself. I am so very fortunate. But I wrestle with anxiety. I believe that no-one cares.

Having gratitude does not negate experience, nor does it negate consciousness. Social justice, the core patterning that makes a human society functional and purposeful to the benefit of all in that society, is the action of living well. When I know that I may lose everything on any given day, I find myself agitated. I think of refugees, of children caught in other people's wars, and my heart aches for them. So much distress. I am told by well-meaning people not to think about the things over which I have no control, but I know that there, but for the grace of Goddess, go I. I am told to trust the future, to trust that everything will be okay, but all my actions and energies are directed at ensuring the future can be trusted to exist, for myself and for my children. I ask, what do I trust? My honesty? My integrity? My compassion? Will that put food in my children's mouths?

I am a single mother because I choose to be. I have chosen twice now, because I was no longer prepared to experience emotional abuse, or endure a *practical* relationship. The wife as prostitute. The silencing. The stealing of my self-worth. I was the stay-at-home parent in both my relationships at the time when they ended. My last job was in the UK when I was 25 years old, and since I've just turned 50, this means that I have not engaged in *paid* employment for 25 years. I am a writer, I practise art and very occasionally make a little money from those things. I am very fortunate and have gratitude for the abundance of my life, for the fact that I am a single mother.

The first time that I became a single mother was after the birth of my daughter. I remained so for six years. The second time I became a single mother was when my daughter became sexually active, over four years ago. I read that in Victorian England a man could easily purchase a 13 year old girl's virginity for £5.00. That prostitution was a way for women to earn 'good money.' That prostitutes were divided into three categories, the poor, the independent and the high class. That they were all commodities to be purchased and sold, discarded at whim.

I wonder about this as I cook my breakfast. My heart rate goes up. I do not know how this world can be this world in which I live. Because I am very fortunate. How can people use each other so?

I made a fundamental choice on both occasions of becoming a single mother, and that was to ally myself with my daughter against my partner. In a patriarchy this constitutes a betrayal. So be it. Of course my other children were included in that decision. They, as I perceive, are an extension of me, of *mother*. We all come from mother. But it was the growth of my female child into the world that taught me most about my own experience. Of course.

Today the sunlight stings. The world in still radiance probes relentlessly into dark rooms bolted against knowledge and my body, weighed down with the mechanisms of life, feels bound. My heart, so loud against my pillow, could be a line of youths pounding a hard road to war. It is the time signature of my mortality. What strength have I left to hold to the cliff face, when below the ocean is a maw and I have no wings? That still radiance in those glossy leaves, the little swallow on the post, my hair tangled on a pillow in a cold bed (where my dreams, nonetheless, are warm) are like paintings, the still life to give glimpse of the particular. I close my eyes against the sun and see

the brilliant shape of my blindness. It is a key and the
dark rooms are broken open, that still radiance
explodes and floods like the ocean, in, irrevocably in,
and that oceanic gush carries me into the world below
the world.

I want to write that *a beautiful flower grows there*, but I can't quite, not just yet.

The experience of being a single mother for the second time around reached an all-time low during the debilitating process of separating from a ten year relationship. This was also a process of learning to believe what the law said was my right to receive a proportion of the assets, including superannuation, of the economic aspect of the partnership of which I had been a part. I remember weeping when the lawyer told me that in such legal matters, full time motherhood was considered equal to full time paid employment. I felt relief amidst my distress. How fortunate I was, me, a single mother in patriarchy, acknowledged in this way. And yet the damage had been done. I was confused, afraid and ashamed.

As a single mother in patriarchy I have learned that I must not trust, I must consider my future. And as a single mother in patriarchy, I must live with the experience of being an inconvenience. An irritation.

In this way I learned the complications of patriarchal relationships, of ownership and entitlement. I learned about certain ideas of power. Food, shelter, money and sex. The mother impulse to give, share and provide, to teach, did not extend beyond the circle of my arms. How is mother to care for her children, engage in meaningful social activities as a mature adult, and even improve her circumstances when she is unsupported? She may even be seen as a threat to other women, because patriarchy's favourite means of oppression is to divide and conquer, through violence and misogyny, usually both. Internalise misogyny in women, make them hate themselves and each other. It makes female relationships difficult, it makes male-female relations difficult, but in a patriarchy there will always be prostitutes to fill the void, prostitutes who are often single mothers, too. In a patriarchy, a single mother must at least be useful beyond what she does to ensure that her children grow as whole and functional members of society, which in a patriarchy means that she must ensure that her children are sufficiently anaesthetised to be able to conform and take their place in the appropriate hierarchies, that they are not whole, not functional.

My thoughts sound wretched and bitter to myself. I am a loving person. I am creative, a wild fire and a sweet bloom. I am rage and grief. I am replete with compassion. I look on social media and read a brief account of a glossy erotic bondage performance that has evolved from an ancient Samurai practise of humiliating captives. People applaud it for being so elegant, so tidy, so beautiful. I have a panic attack. It reminds me again that I live in a world where violence is being systematically eroticised. Where what is normalised is made moral, and that false morality has nothing to do with kindness or compassion or service to others, but is abstraction. Convenience. And abstraction dulls perception. I live in a patriarchal world which is a pornographic world. I am a single mother in a pornographic, patriarchal world. I refuse to be a prostitute or a wife, because that is what I choose, and I have gratitude for the capacity to make that choice. I am so very fortunate, unlike many who must choose only to survive. *There but for the grace of Goddess, go I.* For the veils between are thin, and no-one wishes to care for my children without expecting something in return.

The day unfolds. I read. I compose my Art History essay about the concept of beauty and how it has changed, or has not changed. I will not feel guilty for having intelligence. I will not be ashamed of my vision for a better world. I will not be reduced to passive gratitude. My gratitude will be a wild fire. I will do what I am able, and grieve, and grow as I must. For my great grandmother who could not choose, and for my daughter who now walks before me, I will choose.

'You are weary,' she said, as she gazed at me,
'and the journey for you not done.
You must go on still, and weep your tears,
'til the thread of your life is spun.'

She held my thread by the light of the dawn
and it gleamed so fair and thin;
and the sea came in to wash the hem
of the gown that I travelled in.'

All poetry and prose by Louise M. Hewett
August 22, 2016

F* you, babies

Marianne Evans-Lombe

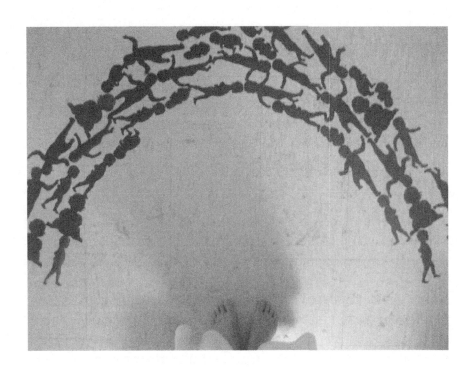

F* you, babies, an in-progress performance that embodies the the feelings of constraint and restraint that mark my experience of mothering my children.

F* you, babies is a project created to hold space for us to give voice to the negative aspects of mothering - for women who have given birth to a child or adopted one and those who have not.

Participants are sent an email with a series of questions. They can answers any or all of the questions; or choose to write an essay instead. Participants then record their answers or essays for the performance soundtrack. The participants are given the option of having their name added to project materials or remaining anonymous.

The live performance aspect of *F* you, babies* is my response to this space and embodies the feelings of constraint and restraint that mark my experience of mothering my children.

I drew, cut-out, painted and ironed over 300 silhouettes of seven different babies. The babies are made from a plastic shower curtain. I will dance my frustration with these babies as I move in, struggle with, and confront the process of mothering.

F* you, babies is accompanied by original music composed for it by Stacey Barelos, and the voices of the women who participated in the project.

I will perform *F* you, babies* four times. There will be one performance on each of the dates my four children were born: December 28, May 22, June 15, and September 23.

http://www.bodydrawings.org/in-progress/f-you-babies

My Daughter

Marianne Evans-Lombe

Two things
I held you
I cried
I held you
You cried
All I could do
was paint you
Those strokes
became you
That color
becomes you
My regret
is not
you

For Rosa

Marianne Evans-Lombe

You my small and
beautiful
The one I didn't
forsee
The one I could not
see
Because of that
and
this
I honed my intuition
on your being

One Tough Mother

Marianne Evans-Lombe

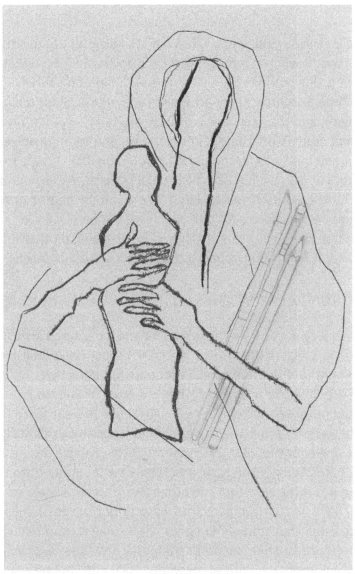

Vine charcoal and graphite on paper.

It's Time To Fight Back Against the Systemic-Historical Violence of Male Governance

Nile Pierce

BEYONCE THINKS GIRLS RUN THE WORLD. I like her optimism, but it's off-base. If women ran the world – if it was really true that we run the fucking world – 3.5 million female children in Turkey wouldn't be in contractually-arranged rape relationships (child 'marriage'), and the pregnant girls of Boko Haram wouldn't have been abducted, impregnated, left alone to fend for themselves, and shamed by their community. We would be fucking safe from rape, from abuse, from misogynist social policies. We wouldn't be scared for the safety of our children. We would be able to make more and better choices for ourselves and our families. We wouldn't be marginalized and shamed for enjoying motherhood. We wouldn't be fucking *oppressed* like biblical fucking slaves.

We are in the fucking wilderness.

If you're a woman and you decide to have a baby, good luck. It's not easy to navigate the array of social (let's just call it 'bullshit' for the moment) bullshit and expectations surrounding the experience. If you're a single mother, the level of bullshit is increased ten-fold and navigating it all is much more intense because you are alone. That being said, It's not always difficult being a single mother. But for a vast majority of single moms, it's fucking hard. And it's lonely, and isolating. Women that have the privilege of having a partner (whether that partner is male or female) have *help*. This means they have *financial* help in most instances, and that kind of help goes a long way toward relieving a lot of pressure and helping other things in their lives, such as physical and mental health for example. Having someone else around that you can trust to care for your children when you are sick or tired, is an amazing thing. You can *rest*. They can rest. However, many of us don't have that privilege. We just go and go and go and go. All of us have to make difficult decisions to make things work financially. Sometimes to the detriment of our relationships with our children and ourselves. We women have to make choices. But the choices that we are 'presented' with by society are not fair. Not by a fucking long shot.

The truth is, we are *controlled*. By men. I'm not going to waste time dragging in statistics here to prove this point but if you want to google some, feel free. Take a look at the ratios of men to women in positions of power all over the world and you'll get a better idea of how controlled we are. From presidents of countries, to corporations, to town hall and city council boards, we are controlled in every which way imaginable. Because we are rarely in positions of power, men make the majority of decisions that affect our lives in both public and private ways. They rely on their own male understandings of reality when they do this – which is obviously highly problematic considering how many of them are religious fundamentalists and think that the pains of childbirth are our punishment from God for tempting Adam in the garden. This is literally what they think. They also think that we are all objects to be fucked. This is what they think. The porn industry is as successful as it is because our society has normalized its acceptance. Women need to wake the fuck up to what this is doing to us and our daughters. And our sons.

We have children on our own terms. But even when we do, the only options 'offered' to us are options created by men in power. We are not consulted for policy that affects our livelihoods and existence. We are *forced* to pay tax on necessities like tampons and fucking menstrual pads. Our social, sexual, emotional, and financial resources are continually extracted by men in power for their own benefit and it needs to stop. These extractions are violent because they are *forced* and they are against our will and against our intuitive intelligence. *Forced* extractions do not equal choice, just as forced 'sex' does not equal sex – it equals rape. This must stop. Our resources are valuable and we must protect them.

If we have a baby, we are *forced* to return to work. Frustrated with being forced to return to work, we are *forced* to play the capitalist game – which is essentially a misogynist game that places more value on the accumulation of capital than on the building of a strong and healthy society. Enmeshed within this system, rife with a variety of damaging liberal feminisms disguised as progressive politics that are patriarchally oppressive in nature to women, we are *forced* to perform male-sanctioned 'work' and neglect caring for our children. We are *forced* to make 'choices' that hurt. We are *forced* to literally go against our nature and our instincts, to leave our children in the care of strangers who we are not allowed to personally vet; we are *forced* to trust the state and its policies and practices in the governance of our lives and that of our children. We are *forcefully* placed between a rock and a hard place:

   1 Between slaving away in a bullshit capitalist economy that devalues our motherhood and our work at home through a variety of misogynist social mechanisms constructed to oppress and erase us - or -
   2 Staying home and having our maternal work devalued through a variety of misogynist social mechanisms.

WE. ARE. AT. WAR. With ourselves, internally, and with the patriarchal structures of society, externally. We are at war with ourselves internally because the external social mechanisms and forces of misogyny press down upon us, press down upon our minds and our hearts, twisting our emotions, making it hard to know what to do with the 'choices' we are *forced* to accept, realizing that in this system, the 'options' available to us are not really choices after all, and so we are made angry, we are deeply hurting, we are made to feel like we have given up, like we are not contributing enough if we choose to stay at home with our children, we are made to feel like we are weak, non-contributing social leeches, unable to perform like everyone around us, according to male capitalist expectations.

FUCK THAT.

We are not fucking slaves. Not to capitalism, and not to patriarchy. Our children are not pawns to be used in the misogynist accumulation of capital. We are not slaves. Our children are not slaves. We owe it to ourselves and to our daughters and the future of our world to stand up to this systemic-historical violence and take our fucking power back. We will no longer allow male-dominated systems and patriarchal regimes of rationalisation to govern us through oppressive rules, policies, agendas, and misogynist practices. We will no longer allow men to dictate what options are available to us. We will no longer accept male-constructed realities of capitalist 'choice' as the only options on our table. We will no longer tolerate the extraction of our natural resources. We will create our own structures of power and governance. We are going to dismantle this system and make it work for US. We are going to make it work in the name of Goddess, in the names of all of the mothers who have gone before us and been abused, violated, devalued, marginalised, mistreated, raped, maimed, oppressed, and silenced. We are the lifeblood of this world. We have always been. They depend on us. Without us they literally wouldn't exist. They owe it to us to listen. And if they don't, we will fight back.

We will shame them. We will publicly call them out on their bullshit. We will not take 'no' for an answer anymore. We are stronger than what we may appear. We are a force more powerful than any government, policy, or religion.

We are going to change the world.

Heads of Household

Mia Wright

this is what I say to Mr. Murray:
women raised me.
kitchen and classroom women
women seated at the violent chamber
of discipline and reckoning

the men

babysat.
looked, from liquor glasses, on
as best they could —
quiet cigarette misters.

I know what Murray will mutter
about patriarchy.
His pinstripes precede him. Seems his kind
were always at war
for the power of the Father,

their "Daddy's girl" mythology
a random snatch at tenderness
while flexing utilitarianism:
bigger dinner portions, feet up, first crack
at the law

he doesn't like my law,
a woman in stiff jaws and gray curls.

he does not like my wars
fought with clothespins and devotion

he sits, mostly, and stares –
remediless

Minor Assimilations

Mia Wright

our first mother-daughter
chat
will not be a pillowy
body in our laps.
dear creature,

I will not lie to you.
the split between your legs,
that place you been cut,
is neither miracle nor metaphor
and   that much
I wish my mother had told me.

between your feminine   and your femininity
lay a snide whiteness
sleeping   you will nurture it
                                         and slaughter it

all in due time.
right now, you must play
                                     and learn
to learn. one day, sharply dressed
and bristling with reform,

civilized society will present itself
it will stoop at the knee, examine

your eyes
and pinch your softness   for bruises

until you callus.

this is   called growing up.

Another Ghost Father

Mia Wright

tree-brown legs
and hard shoes

I won't claim
he is not more
than this.
but to give you a woman's
shatterless lungs

for breathing safely
in this world
I could not
permit him
to be less.
this is not that
kind of confession:

dear and stuttering maternal,
i've gone off now
and had myself
a child.
the object of this game
is not to sustain
another ghost
(father)

my potential for
wrong
is the only parallel for my
love.

the only condition of my
love
is the oxygen to give it in

unobstructed

More Honesty

Mia Wright

this is what I will tell you about
(him):

one day while the sun
colored me in silver bars,   I put my hand
where it didn't belong.
this is not how you
were conceived.
what I knew was irrelevant.
what I know was   that I knew the way

it couldn't happen.
I want to say there was
heat and mysticism.   a sparkle.
a divination.

what difference does
begetting in love
make, anyway?

       daughter,

you were born
and born again
everyday
in the love I created

       to be stronger

Heteronormativity and the Single Parent

Jacinda Townsend

I. **It's 2012,** and I've just moved to Indiana with my children, aged two and seven. Jill[16], one of the mothers at my older daughter's school, a woman who my older daughter euphemistically refers to as having *personality*, has invited me to her divorce support group. About this, I am perfectly squeamish. My divorce was not a hard thing. I daresay that by the time I actually filed, it had become a life dream. The most terrible part of it was its taking so long— almost three years. I'd been finished with marriage, emotionally, for almost a decade before mine was legally over. I'd been finished not only with my marriage but with the very idea of marriage for probably half that time. It's 2012, I'm happily divorced, and I don't need a support group. A celebratory parade, perhaps, after three years of fighting to protect my children's future, but not a support group.

When I arrive at Jill's home, her newly minted ex-husband is outside, spraying their children's wooden swing set with a garden hose, and I think, for a divorce support group, this is an interesting touch. *Hello*, he waves, gripping his hose, sending spray down the slide, and I wave back. I've interacted with him only at school dropoff and pickup, but I do know that he seems to have less *personality* than Jill. I smile at him as I cross Jill's carport to enter her side door. *Hello*.

Jill is a former New Yorker whose figure is still pre-pregnancy toned, as if in defiance of her decade of being a mother. She is brash and abrasive, like no New Yorker I met in the eight years I

---

16 Not her real name.

myself lived there, but rather like a caricature of a New Yorker, and when I enter her house, she turns her head so sharply her brunette curls shake. "He has to do all the yard work until we sell this house," she says, proudly answering a question I hadn't planned to ask. "I had that written in the decree."

I sit down and introduce myself to the one other person who has shown up: a dressed-down fortysomething whose hair is platinum blond except for two inches of grayish black roots she has tried to hide with a bandana. It turns out she, too, has been divorced for almost a year. I'm hoping the group of us will chat about coparenting schedules, or the logistical hurdles of shuttling our children to extracurricular activities now that we're outnumbered. Instead, after ten minutes of sharing our backstories, the support group meeting turns into a dating strategies war room.

"I'm not dating," I tell them.

"Oh, you just need time," they both say, almost in unison.

"No, I'm never dating. That time in my life is over, I've decided. It's a relief, actually."

This they pretend to understand, though their faces soften into skepticism. They continue talking and I continue listening, but when Jill launches into a tearful account of how she skipped her annual family photo because she felt she and her two daughters were "no longer a family," I feel the urge to interject. "But you are a family," I say. "You're a family of three instead of a family of four."

This time, Jill's face hardens. She looks at me as if I'm a squirrel. I finish my tea, stay another polite ten minutes, and then gather my keys and excuse myself. As in literally, excuse. "My daughter has a piano lesson," I lie. It's Sunday.

II. The Oxford English Dictionary defines heteronormativity as "a world view that promotes heterosexuality as the normal or preferred sexual orientation." A more expansive understanding, however, accounts for the body of work of Michael Warner, the social theorist who coined the term: heteronormativity undergirds all sorts of social and economic structures with the pervasive and oft times malignantly exclusionary belief that people fall into distinct yet complementary gender roles, with implications for the nuclear family and society at large. These implications range from tax structures that reward the married, two-parent family to the rising trend of the school daddy-daughter dance.

Heteronormativity, and its pounding insistence that the correct and proper nuclear family consists of two parents, swims against the tsunamic change that modern family structure has seen in the last fifty years. According to the United States Census Bureau, there were 13.7 million single parents in the United States as of 2011 raising 22 million children. The vast majority—82.2%—of these single parents are women, which means that much of the heteronormative outcry against single parenthood involves a good healthy dose of sexism. Spend one week watching mainstream media in the United States and you'll easily gather that single mothers are ruining society. The media, however, reports no corresponding "single dad" problem, even as those households see an increase in number: single fathers, according to mainstream media, are heroes. Saviours. A single dad puts his daughters' hair in a mermaid braid and the video of him doing so goes viral.

The valor of single dads notwithstanding, parental number status is one of the last personal axes that is acceptably open for discrimination. While hateful rhetoric against people based on race, gender, religion, ethnicity, sexual orientation or disability status is widely censured in the West, attacks on single parents come from both the right and the left sides of the political spectrum. Society accepts almost as fact the gambit that the single parent home is inferior to the two-parent home: Republican Ted Cruz, during his now-famous 2013 Senate filibuster against universal healthcare, invoked the spectre of "the struggling single mom... waitressing in a diner" and thus dependent on government benefits.

This trope is, of course, the mythical creation of a patriarchy that feels its relevance disappearing. According to the Census Bureau, only 30% of single mothers (and 18% of single fathers) live below the federal poverty line: that's an awful lot of us who are doing just fine. But Republicans love to trot out the myth of the sad, government-dependent single mother: earlier in 2015, Ron Johnson, another United States Senator, urged the hypothetical single mother to "increase her take-home pay" by finding "someone to support her." In perhaps one of its ugliest manifestations, the myth trots itself out when teens and young adults in the United States perpetrate gun violence, with pundits and commentators decrying the breakdown of the American family, even though Mother Jones reports that almost two-thirds of mass shooters were raised in two-parent homes.

The political left, alas, does not exactly embrace single parenting, though its rhetoric is softer and subtler. "Let's face it," said President Obama himself, during his 2012 campaign for reelection," – a mixed kid from Hawaii born to a single mom is not likely to become president of the United States." In point of fact, George Washington, the very first president of the United States, was raised by a single mother after his father died when he was eleven. Andrew Jackson's father died before the seventh president was even born. Bill Clinton? Thomas Jefferson? Both raised by single mothers.

This prevailing rhetoric, of single parenting as suboptimal lifestyle choice, is far from benign. It informs public opinion and worse, it informs public policy. It molds a country where discrimination based on parental number status is perfectly acceptable. In the middle of my divorce, I decided to take my biracial daughter out of her small private school and move her to a public school district that was the most diverse in town. I looked, then, to rent a duplex in the district, one on an attractive street of duplexes I'd seen near the school itself. The landlord showed me the unit but rejected my application. I asked why. I had perfect credit, I told him. A job teaching at the university. "I don't rent to single-income families," he said.

I was stunned. I called the Illinois Human Rights Commission and learned that this was perfectly legal, and my shock turned to rage. I was paying more in rent in my current duplex than this landlord was asking. I'd just gotten an advance from my publisher that could have paid the entire year's worth of rent.

But I was a "single-income family." To this man, my finances weren't even worth further interrogation.

III. I did not grow up, not really, in a two-parent household. My own parents separated the first time when I was a toddler, and then remarried each other when I was a ten-year-old. The eight years that I was raised by a single parent were my more formative years; they were years of peace, years of idyll. My mother had a very singular vision for my childhood—she wanted academic excellence first and foremost. Her most potent desire was for me to be the valedictorian of my high school. I took it a bit further, and was accepted into Harvard at the age of sixteen.

Which wouldn't have happened had I been raised in the two-parent household in which I began life. My mother, a rather bohemian high school English teacher, and my father, a rather uptight sales executive at General Electric, were ill-suited for each other. Their remarriage, when I was ten, and their subsequent divorce, more than a decade later, were marked by the kind of violent nastiness I do not like to recall even through words on paper. Conflict was a norm in my two-parent home; beneath the surface of even the best days in my two-parent family, there was tension. When I arrived home from the prom, I opened my front door to find clothes that had been thrown, in a rage, all around the foyer; I shut the door on the whole scene and bid my prom date goodnight on the front steps. My parents' ideas of parenting were quite different, even when my sister and I were small children; there was very little unified vision about things like bedtime or piano lessons or grade skipping. Though I would come to love my parents again, post-divorce, as people who found the most happiness in being single, I remember the years they were my married parents as some of my most miserable.

My children, similarly, would tell you that they did not know much enduring calm when I was married to their father. They endured much screaming, much throwing of objects. They endured a household where their two parents had radically differing views on parenting. Now that their father and I are divorced, they have two different households to turn to, two different sets of rules about life, two wholly different world views, one no less valuable than the other. That my ex-husband and I need not try to make these opposing views of parenting coalesce is critical to our children's well-being.

83

Indeed, as fellow single mother and writer Rene Denfeld recently told me, "There are times sole parenting is optimal. Not second best: optimal. And no one wants to admit it." Denfeld points to benefits such as more responsible and independent children who contribute more to the home. Along with these more intangible benefits to single parenthood, there are many that can be quantified. As a single mother I am able to take my two children to Morocco often, for months at a time; their father's schedule would never permit such lengthy family vacations. I have sole decision-making power over my children's religious, educational, and health needs; all of the energy I was once spending trying to manage a parenting relationship with another adult, I can now spend on my children.

Yet even as my children test into the gifted program, perform well in their extracurricular activities, and grow into kind, loving, elegant young women, my home is judged inferior. Mia Birdsong and Nicole Rodgers, in their essay "Another One Percent White Privilege," refer to this as nuclear parent privilege. "We live in a country," they write, "where this increasingly uncommon family arrangement gets respect and support that is denied to the rest of us." Birdsong and Rodgers point to tax breaks and employment policies, medical care and media representation, and the urging of bipartisan political groups to focus on an agenda of "removing the barriers to marriage." "Because we are blind to the ways in which our society benefits nuclear families," they write, "when they thrive, we believe it is because there is something intrinsically better about them."

Indeed, the gap in wealth and employment between the single-mother-led household and the single-father-led household is but one telltale sign that structural inequality, rather than family structure itself, is responsible for any statistical difference in outcome between children parented in two-parent versus single-parent families. While 76% of custodial single mothers are gainfully employed according to those Census Bureau statistics, more than 85% of custodial single fathers are. And while 30% of single mothers live below the poverty line, only 18% of single fathers do. This has little to do with family structure and everything to do with gender discrimination and a glaring lack of pay equity in the United States.

I feel fortunate to have grown up in a mostly single-family home. The benefits of my mother's sole parenting were enormous. More than that, I feel fortunate because I never quite received this message that society has tried to pound into me as an adult, this message that a family structure that a majority of women will find themselves in at some point during their parenting is somehow inferior. Now that I'm a single parent myself, I can happily and easily celebrate what other people discourage. I can understand the absolute advantages of my situation and see it clearly, unfettered with societal views.

"What do we really know about any familial structure?" asks the writer Cole Lavalais, in her forthcoming novel *Summer of the Cicadas*. "They're all like raindrops. Unique and different. Therefore resistant to reduction."

Feral Mothering

Lesley 'Orion' Johnson

She comes to an abyss,
Across it she saw a warm dwelling & realized how tired she'd grown.
How much she'd forgiven.
A ways down the cliff edge she saw what looked like a bridge
It's faint and dark where it crossed, she could barely make it out
But she imagined
It connecting
To shelter.
She stepped into what seemed only shadow but she just believed so much
Seemed simple,
innocent love to home,
Slipping.
She tracked back.
She found her footing again
& felt foolish
Thinking it so easy to cross the abyss
Almost like a trick someone else left
She walked further
Thinking their must be a way.
Another bridge seemingly built by a legacy
Grand
Stately,
It seemed a formality of performance was demanded to cross,
A secret courtesy expected
A lock,

A gate.

On the other side of the bridge she saw flashes of light like cameras flashing.

A gust of thick wind pushed her to the gates & in her ears she heard,

'You're perfect.' 'You're just what we need.' 'I want to be you!!

A frothing pulled that she struggled to hold her ground within

Sliding across & down to the limb, the trunk, reaching to hold on,

Crawling she pulled from the force of the locked door.

Shuddered from the pull of it.

Vomited from being seen as things she never knew herself to be.

Shaking she followed the tree line along the cliff,

Passing what appeared more innocent shadow bridges

She continued,

Less interested in falling

It becomes colder & her toes begin to numb,

Then there

Almost blue

A frozen bridge

Like a tidal wave of power

Still in time

solid

Muscles tight & tense joints

Her foot taps to test the ice

& eases up the ample arch

As she skates the bridge narrows & constricts until she's walking across a fine line

Black below

& white dividing it

Where has she gotten herself

She falls back hardly able to breath

Gasping as lightly as she can
Tears burn her eyes & she scoots gently back
Slowly
Unsure she wants to try again
Wishing she never had
She makes it back to the edge
Before the abyss
She collapses to her side
& curls into a ball
Staring
Across a schism
So dark
& hidden
She can't see the hut
In the darkness
She forgets why it was ever
So alluring.
She's tired now
Right here.
Just stay.
Feral.

Mushroom Genitals

Lesley 'Orion' Johnson

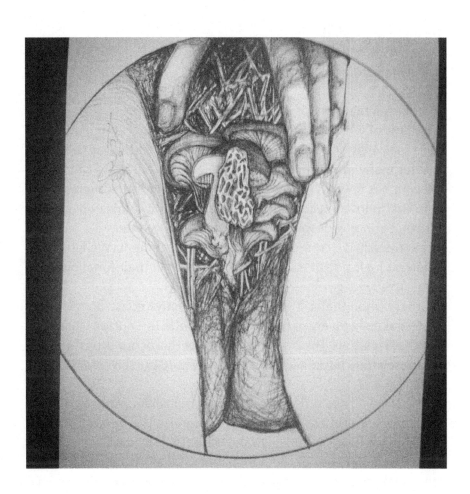

Deconstructing Parents

Lesley 'Orion' Johnson

the oak tree that made an acorn.

the mom & the dad.

the legal guardians.

In order to create enough wealth to support a child to the standards of white supremacy, one must work more hours than it takes to give attention to and raise a child. Since this has been the case for many many generations we are children raising children still with not enough time to let a child relax and trust themselves in an environment... To anticipate this deficiency and keep our affluence running despite the growth of culture inter generationally we create structures of displacement. We label the children's logical restlessness to a deficiency in their functioning.

Another option that is evolving in the collective consciousness is an idea of collectively parenting to dismantle the nuclear families habits of isolation. The implosion point of this conundrum is that we are severely backed up on being parented ourselves.

Essentially we have not learned to trust our relationship to the earth because it is less exhausting to diagnose the symptoms than to realize we have no language for maturity and humility intertwined. Because of the humiliation of realizing we are collectively children, biological birthing vessels commonly known as mothers take the brunt of displaced personal growth. This means mother figures are expected to birth the maturity of all of their peers along with the age of their child. Uniformly in a nuclear family dynamic all fault and responsibility falls on the dichotomy of masculinity and femininity, which has proven again & again to be unsustainable. In queer family, all fault falls on the gender spectrum that the individual biological guide represents which ultimately means one person holds the entire spectrum of gender for the whole community. Our children are not only our children they are the next generation of our species. How do we step into collective parenting with the understanding that we are collectively holding everyone's developmental trauma?

Masculinity Mothering

Lesley 'Orion' Johnson

People always say,
'Uhhhnnn. Why didn't she leave that dude if he was beating her?
Stupid.'
They don't tell you
that it takes her whole life
To go
& she's still trying to give her life to her mom in honor.
This isn't a negotiation.
If violence comes up,
Boom
Woman
Go.
Just drop it.
Just drop your life
& leave it behind
Don't take that.
They don't tell you
You can't run your whole life
Someday you'll be blamed for it
Well actually
MRA's do say that sometimes,
It's casually that blatant.
They don't tell you she's already been working on her mom's &
her gramma's trauma for getting slapped in the mouth for holding
her worth to his ego.

They say,
'Some people just like that.'
Fuck you.
No.
I will define myself.
& one day my story won't scare the shit out of me because my environment won't reflect that.
I am mirroring you society.
Who's the villain now?!
I am.
Not Me.
I'm speakin to patterns as reflection
& yes the time it takes to observe is valid.
Slow that business,
You are not the industry.
You are also this rock & tree.
Take responsibility each moment
Hyper awareness is endurance of the elements of wilderness inside and outside of us.
Just watch your focus
Keep it grounded through the hounding.
We're actually together in this.
I have been polite for too long
This rudeness is a service.
I used to fuck this son of a race car driver entitled kinda dude.
& was my sister as well in genuine moments.
But the first time he saw me naked he noticed some pimples on my butt
& he wrote a poem about it.
Saying how beautiful I was with little speckles of nutrient deficiencies on my behind.

Saying how he'd love to massage the toxins out of me
& I realized how on an auctioning block I live.
Later he tried to choke the toxins out of me, then scare the toxins
out of me with a knife
Displacing significant responsibility for the why the toxins were in
me to begin with.
I tried to homestead with these older white hippies 'like me'
& they weren't sure.
One of the elder matriarchs of nor cal new age mothering checked
my tongue when I got to her farm. Like a goat.
She didn't have much feedback and sorta stared blankly like I
wasn't of value.
They say,
We weren't bad to you
what are you talking about
preposterous!
Invisible.
These are ancestor settlers y'all.
This is our legacy
of the auctioning block
folding in on us
As it has been the whole time.
My brain is scarring.
Yes it is building just like the muscles in my fascia.
White supremacy is the only contrary brain damage.
It's rancid culture.
All else is fertile organic evolution of a being.
Masculinity mother our self.
Settlers.

No Bragging Rights
Patty Kay

I LIKE TO PRETEND that it never happened. But three children are the living proof that, indeed, it was real. I won't wake up one day to a different reality. I try to not think about it. Any examination of conscience just brings back a lot of self-doubt and oodles of guilt. And the distinct feeling that somehow I will try to fashion my explanation of things in some self-serving way. I am not innocent. But I am not totally guilty either. I am still confused.

There is a 1944 movie named *Gaslight*, based on Patrick Hamilton's 1938 play, *Gas Light*. The film starred Ingrid Bergman as a wife whose husband, played by Charles Boyer, manipulated her into thinking she was insane. One form of ambient abuse is called gaslighting after that movie. The Urban Dictionary defines ambient abuse as "a form of intimidation or psychological abuse... where false information is presented to the victim, making them doubt their own memory, perception and quite often, their sanity." I was gaslighted.

But before I go into all of that, I would like to give you a brief history of my mental state before I was bamboozled. I can't say that I wouldn't have gotten sucked in otherwise, but I'm pretty sure it didn't help that I was operating as a tainted soul who had something to prove.

I got pregnant as a teenager. Abortion was illegal then, even though I knew rich girls who'd done it. I was part of a Roman Catholic family where the shock and horror of my condition was much ballyhooed and I was deemed the black sheep of the family. I had little say-so on how to proceed since I was a minor. I either had to get married or give my baby up to my sister to raise. Neither was a great choice, but I couldn't see a life of pretending that my child was a niece or a nephew. So I married and promptly miscarried after my rather ideal life had been totally disrupted. A divorce followed, once again sullying the family name. Strike two. No one in my family had ever divorced either.

It took a while, but I thought I had gotten over all that. My first marriage had come and gone without too much trauma. It was just me who was scarred because I "let down" my kin. My surface-self had become brash and sassy and fairly successful in a professional sort of way. And there was something rather exotic about being a young divorcee. Men were never a problem to attract. But my soul ached at having upset things and I was resolved to never have a baby outside of marriage, and to never divorce again. It took me 16 years before I was willing to give marriage another try. I had to. My biological clock was making a whole lot of noise!

I lived with the man for a few years before we got married. I sort of took him in as one would do with an orphaned child. And I always thought of him as a child. I never would have expected that he was so devious. I didn't give him that much credit! But I was sincere in my resolve to marry and be the good wife and hopefully good mother. While I didn't expect any real closeness from him, I convinced myself that I could spend the rest of my life being amused by him.

Things were peachy at first. My life proceeded as usual except that I had a focus for my doting. He had just come out of rehab when we hooked up. It became my mission in life to see that he stayed away from drugs. And there's all that courting stuff that one seems to have energy for. Play. All play. And I enjoyed that. I had been on my own for a while and liked having someone to recreate with. So things were going smoothly and I thought I was in charge. Only after the fact can I see how that wasn't the case. I mean, I was the one who worked at a steady job and paid the bills while he hunted and fished most of the time "so-he-wouldn't-do-drugs" (which became the guiding force in my life for a long time!)

We got married by a Justice of Peace and I had my first child before our one-year anniversary. Being the best possible parent I could be became my focus and he was no longer the center of my attention. And that was when his machinations became more overt. Where it had been that I "took care" of him at, what I thought, was my own volition, he now demanded it verbally. Mysterious events became more frequent. He began to bully me. Loudly. And I never thought much about it. I just thought it was my life, I could handle it.

Another child 18 months later. The OB asked me if I wanted to be fixed then. I did. Two children and a grown baby were all I could handle, thank you. But my husband said, "no." I don't know why his opinion mattered or why it prevailed. But I do know that I was in way over my head even then. I shut down. I blamed it on postnatal depression. I stopped talking and I couldn't sleep. And I committed criminal acts.

Prior to then, his attacks had been on my behavior. I wasn't spending enough time tending to his needs and stuff like that. Things I thought I'd tended to were not handled even though I thought I'd taken care of them. After child two, the attacks were on my person. I was fat. (I was a size six!) I was stupid. I was irresponsible. I began to think I hadn't known him near long enough for him to hate me that much! He began to force sex on me. And I was pregnant again in short order.

I was totally bonkers by the time my third child was born. I was tending to babies of all sizes, juggling work and parenthood, covering up my crimes, still trying to prove myself worthy of belonging to my own birth family, and generally ragged with all the plates I was juggling. I was sleeping even less than before, trying to wrack my brain about what I should do. By now, the abuse had become physical. And when I somehow stood up to him for myself, he'd hurt the children. Not physically, just doing spiteful things; giving them soul-crushing insults all the while assuring them that their mother was too crazy to ever be of any use to them. I was what was wrong with them. He was the cool parent who made everything okay.

Tons happened once I confessed. My case was put on hold for a few years until the statute of limitation was about to run out and I was prosecuted and sent to prison. I lost my job, the abuse intensified, the whole world thought me completely corrupt and that poor, sweet man I'd married was a saint for putting up with me. Believe it or not, I still was working and supporting us. Just the job changed. But he was the hero and I was the villain. Now my children were hearing how evil I was. I was a liar and a thief and not worthy of their affection. And he started to use drugs again. I think he'd been doing that for years, only now he wasn't even trying to hide the fact.

I got a 16-month federally mandated time-out. The only good thing I can say about the judicial system in the United States is that I had some time not being harassed by my husband. Most of the women I met in prison had never been as safe and secure as the walls there made them. The time, for me, was a blessing. I learned that I was abused. I never even thought that before. I had believed it was all me. And here I'm not trying to blame anyone. I take responsibility for my actions. But I'm not alone in being responsible. I was not myself. I had a lot of help being nuts. But that break in the constant badgering helped me resolve to truly leave prison behind when I left, and spend the rest of my life trying to undo the damage done to my children. I had to get back to them and get them away.

It took many years before I was able to escape being under my husband's thumb. I'm all too familiar with the walls that are put up at having to check that box about being convicted of a crime. Getting a job was tough. Getting any kind of assistance was tougher. But I got away eventually. I was having to work sixty-hour weeks to keep a roof over our heads. I never really got to be a Momma. But the kids were out of there. And I tried to be fair. They were allowed to see their father as long as he was sober. It was not unusual for me to have to bring them food for the infrequent occasions he was sober enough to see them. Then nothing for a few years. He had another rehab interment and maybe he was seeing them when I was at work or something. But I was out of the loop for that time. I was too busy trying to get by.

Nearly everyone has heard of Hurricane Katrina that devastated New Orleans. I live in southwest Louisiana and we had begun taking in refugees from that storm when we were hit with Hurricane Rita. We were mandated to evacuate and I had made plans to travel to another city with a nephew I trusted. My older son told me he would not leave town without his father. I unhappily acquiesced.

After we were allowed to return, the apartment complex I lived in was condemned. I had already told FEMA we were okay, so when the owners decided they had the opportunity to upgrade and no longer be Section 8 housing, I was put at the bottom of the list for shelter. All of my siblings in town had their own homeless children to tend to. I had been promised a Habitat for Humanity house before the storm, so I thought, "a few months is all I need before my house is built!" So to keep the kids together with me, I agreed to stay with their father.

I am very fearful of that man. My younger sister had tried to take my children away from me when I was incarcerated. I wasn't about to be apart from them again. So I guess I have fears even greater than his words and fists could instill. Now his obsession with hunting and fishing had been replaced with 12-step-o-mania. I don't want to knock a program that has helped so many, but too much of a good thing is not that healthy even for that. It was not rare to have addicts (who were far more dangerous than any of the convicts I'd been associated with) sitting in his living room (the make-shift sleeping quarters for four people), eating the food I had bought and prepared for my children, talking about what an unfair world it was that wouldn't let them be high all the time. All that in front of my children! I paid rent and utilities too. But he was able to act as though we were not there and go on with his 'recovery' all the same.

The place I worked had been totally destroyed by the storm. We were kept on the payroll and worked out of make-shift facilities for more than a year. Work was a place I could be where that man was not. I was there a whole lot. The kids had their friends whose homes they frequented. I doubt the father ever knew where we were!

The few months I had expected to wait before I got a place of my own had turned into 18 months. I finally got my house. My 17-year-old daughter had been kicked out by her father. But my sons and I moved into the new house even before we had time to take our furniture out of storage! What's one floor compared to another? My daughter had managed to get her own place by then, so she didn't join us. She just wanted some peace before she graduated from high school.

I thought that – with this new house – I could finally get on my feet again. But my husband was still sniffing around. I started having panic attacks, experienced a hospitalized meltdown later, and soon realized I wasn't back to myself yet. And here I could tell you some dark things about Big Pharma and psychotropic drugs, but that's a whole other story. Some soul searching and good counselling led me back to school and I felt like I was ready to become me again. Another hurricane just weeks into the school year shut school down for a week. The anxiety caused my blood pressure to go wild. It was so high that the doctors thought I may need a heart stint. A heart catheter was scheduled. I had a stoke a week after the procedure was performed. I was paralyzed. So long to the man who'd given me so much grief. He didn't want any part of a physically impaired woman. And so long to my education. My body didn't work, my brain didn't work and I literally had no voice.

I can walk again. In fact, I'd say I'm 70% better after five years recovering. I tire very easily, and I can't run. In fact, I have trouble standing for long and I still "thud" when I go down to sit. I got Social Security Disability while I was still bedridden. I got that because I had been crazy enough to be considered disabled, not because I couldn't walk. But it came in handy because I couldn't work at all then.

I had to ask for child support as part of my getting assistance. My husband paid one year of support for my one child who was still in high school. The process of getting child support was only possible for me because a social worker took over my case. I was required to take my husband to court by the state. Fortunately, he didn't even bother to show up. I had a mini-breakdown afterwards that alarmed my psychologist. I've never talked about how afraid of that man I am before now. The shrink saw it on court day!

I am still afraid of him. We are still legally married because, frankly, I don't want to pay for one more thing that might benefit him. And I don't want to incur his wrath. Further, I have no faith in my judgement where men are concerned as my experience thus far discourages me from trying to form a new relationship. My children still think I'm a little nuts, but I've managed to get to a place that lets me know they love me. My life is very small, but I really have no complaints. I survived.

Dearest Great Granddaughter of Mine

Auriol Hays

I HOPE YOU WILL FIND these letters useful somehow. I wonder who you are. Are you a musician or an artist like your grandmother? If so, dear faraway child, I hope my prayers leap across this page and find you safe, free and courageous above all. I doubt that I am the first musician in our line. I often wonder about those who sang before me. Did they dream in sound as I do? Do memories of a time past shadow their steps the way they do mine? Allow me to share a dream of a life past, so you can understand that I had no real choice – even at the very start.

I was facing the end of one life, my sister at my side sobbing as she gently wiped my face for the last time. She tried to keep me there, reminding me of the small and big joys we shared. I wanted to stay, tried to remain for her; yet felt myself drawn... away from her side, my body, until I sat on a bench alone in a park. I waited there until I was guided to a room, a chamber, and felt a hand on my shoulder.

-Come

The moment I entered the room I was encircled, bands of colour wove into each other. Vibrating, radiating life. He guided my hand toward the bands of colour that enveloped me and in that moment I remembered. I was seeing Music. A Tuscan sun infused chord of light, spilt sunlight in every dimension and arched onwards, outwards, through folds of all my lives...

-Close your eyes. Listen

And then I heard it... my voice woven around, between, underneath the thick band of colour. My voice was the source of the colour I saw. All the frequencies that anchored my body to the earth and those I loved: songs I wrote, sung, thought of, the heavy panting of our love making, the bubbling voices of my children, sister, my godchildren, his sonorous laughter, deep brown sorrow, hope, tenderness; every emotion that infused my music. He placed my hand on his heart and gently whispered...
This is how your music always made me feel.

Even now I can recall with vividness that dream, his love and the stillness it brought. A stillness that allowed me to sing – freely in that life. I woke from that dream and knew in that instant that I would leave my first husband Claud, and search for Music and that man whose face I did not see; the man who gifted me with stillness. Little did I know the toll it would take, but more of that when you are ready, or perhaps when I am ready to part with those stories hmm?

Many years later, a professional musician, I would recall that dream as I stepped on stage. I envisioned every sound, every nuance finding its way to my audience. I would elongate my notes, my words and offer them pearlescent green waves caught in the afternoon sun to luxuriate in. Or hurl rolling thunder, my notes staccato and sharp, rising and falling unexpectedly, crackling electric blue, to awaken, arouse. But Music written for my Darling-Love radiated light, note by note.

I sent him music bathed in cerulean that raked his curly brown hair on nights when he could find no peace. Galaxies of admiral blue swarmed around his fingers, his temples, when at work. In the early mornings music the colour of a dandelion breeze, strangely wonderful; ice cream in the hands of a three year old

when the sun burnt the brightest. And when he sat down to read his paper, or sip his tea, wisps of sea-foam green relieved his weary shoulders. Music written for my Darling-Love, swayed with an intoxicating delirium that spoke of love and love alone.
I shared this dream with my Mother.

My child, we come from a long line of dreamers...

I hope, faraway child that you dream. And not dismiss them as most do. Inside those dreams are colours, music and stories of such richness and depth. Remember them as best you can and find whatever truth resides there. I will leave you with this: May you be blessed above all not with music, but with a mother who knows the curvature of your dreams, the arc of your desires, and stands beside you, prayers in hand. And if Grace finds you, may you be that Mother...

Save the Children

Shamecca Long

I am not afraid of these conversations.
As a matter of fact,
I'm armed.
Weaving a weaponry of
Knowledge.
Self-defense.
Voice detonating hiding places.
You will not find solace
In silenced homes.
Broken heart.
Single parent shame.
There's a name for women like me.
Women who've swallowed
Their tongues
To allow their mothers to live.
Women whose bodies
Become wasteland.
Punching bag.
Toys.
For the men who never become men.
I am waiting for you.
I have a daughter.
I am waiting for you.
I have a daughter.
It is waiting for you.
Near my daughter.
Nestled where you slip into dreams.
Prepared to split your body open
Should your mind

Desire the innocence
I have been robbed of.

Rebirth

Shamecca Long

15 hours ago
These walls were battlegrounds.
Your father and I
Bulls.
Trying to cultivate a flower
In an environment
Thick with toxicity.
Each step was volatile
Exhausting life's blessings
By engaging in ambush.
His pride.
How it buckled under the heaviness
Of cynicism.
My skin
How his hands sculpted rainbow hues.
Yet,
On this day
This pain
A water break
Brought the type of flood
That seals you inside.
Your first breath an uprising.
A warning shot
That the only fight to ensue
Is the fight to improve
The fight to remove
Transatlantic gashes.
Your presence is sutures.
Little fingers outlining the fullness of Life

This love is militant.
Stretching like eons.
She knows I'm not perfect
Yet sees no asymmetry.
Says mommy and unicorns
Are made of the same magic.
A gift with the reminder
That despite me being war torn
She chose me.
Commanding ceasefire into existence.
I'm forever grateful
How she spared my life.

After the Heartbreak

Shamecca Long

To my daughter.
Locked behind
What seems to be opportunity.
Having interviewed
For role of past girlfriend.
Drowning in new heartbreak.
Trying to be better lifeguard.
I hear you.
Wishing yourself water.
More life.
More force.
To a dam of a boyfriend.
It is over.
But you are not finished.
Learn how to float
With life
Pummeling your back.
You won't sink.
Don't think
Heartbreak
Equals earthquake.
Your world is not
Split in two.
It has simply removed
A leech.
Please understand
There's no need for
Hand me down love.
It leaves you starved.

Brittle.
Bitter.
Feeding on yourself.
And we know hunger intimately.
Your grandmother
In a 20-year marriage
Experiencing famine.
Her mouth harvests blades.
A love so barren.
Managed to raise 5 children.
Bury 2.
Continue through suffering.
Don't be fooled
A brick house is still hollow.
Resist carbon copy.
Never remove magic
From your bones
For a man versed in
Disappearing acts.
Remember how water
Can be cleansing.
Your water is renewing.
These are the fruits
My mother yields.

The Stigma

Anne Bonnie

"SINGLE MOM" AS DISCRIMINATION is something I don't really care about, even though it definitely exists in Germany. Daily sexism is found full force in the attributions of single mothers and in the political structure.

Tax reduction does not exist and there is not enough financial assistance. Single moms are typically blamed for breaking up the relationship, or they are judged as guilty for not finding a "good father." And for sure, they are guilty for anything that interferes with a father's relationship with their children.

I was raised in a family without men. My great grandmother lost two men in two world wars and my grandmother and mother are divorced.

And so am I.

I experienced my childhood happier without a father. The fathers in my village were dominant and angry. They took too much space for their own needs and were unwilling to see family members' issues. Lots of my female friends are still searching for love and recognition from their daddies as adults. Growing up with fathers who are not willing to learn how to feel or show love is an ongoing problem in heteronormative relations.

Despite problematic family structures, I developed myself freely without being pressed to fulfill a "girlie role" or being daddy's *good girl*.

Nevertheless, I have experienced discrimination as a white, able-bodied woman. Because of the lack of education on my parent's and grandparent's side – and my mother's divorce – I was considered less than good. Typical for "white trash," I became pregnant as a teenager and realized negative ascription as a teenage mom. But the hardest discrimination I suffered was that of being a mother apart from her children.

After breaking up with my husband, I needed to confess to myself that he is better at caring for the kids. I was in the process of breaking up with my family and went to Berlin. Taking my kids with me would have required that I separate them from their social environment and the rest of their family. I did not have a job or apprenticeship and I was willing to go back to school. I needed to organize my new life.

This decision was made for my children. Nevertheless, the corporate judgment of my decision insulted my deeply. From then on, I was considered a bad mother.

During the last few years I have educated myself and feminist theory has helped me to understand a great deal about prejudice.

I was also successfully self-employed and I was working (at least until I burnt out). This break was important and I feel now more and more like a strong and wise woman.

After setting new goals in my life and making some positive steps forward, I became pregnant from a man who uses (without consent) no condom. He came after three pushes. The day-after pill didn't work.

And family drama comes up once more in my life. During my pregnancy and the year afterward, I was completely unstable. The only thing that kept me functional, was my deep trust in myself as a mother. This little human was a gift and he helped me heal my inner wounds.

At once I understood the meaning of being a single mom in a patriarchal society – like a punch in my face!

Valuation of the mother role in patriarchy!

Nobody understood that offering help would have been needed. It is a capitalist construction that mothers alone get all the responsibility. If the biological father is missing, no one takes over to share the responsibility.

My friends call themselves left, social or queer. I start talking about support options during the pregnancy, they kept listening and agreed, but no one offered support.

The construction of social family is often theoretically built in different subcultures. Their own scope of action is still not seen. While people understand the theoretic ideas, they often don´t see their own responsibility to act. People may understand the struggle of a single mom, but they don´t see that they can help to solve or minimize these problems. It´s easier to blame a society then figuring out what can I do...

At the same time, I´ve had many big financial problems. I live on welfare, have debts and paybacks, and once had a reduction of my welfare because I brought some papers in too late. Altogether, I lived on 250€ monthly for more than six months for me and a baby. I lost 16 pounds in the first weeks because I could not buy myself enough food and received compliments for losing weight.

Isolation

The changing and losing of friendships (combined with my financial problems) isolated me completely.

I tried to create a Facebook event called: "Welfare is eating my social contacts" and offered cooking services for 2-5€. The feedback was amazing. I felt like it was important to do this – to show the realities of single moms. But as the event drew closer, I started getting cancellations and lots of "best wishes" to have lots of fun.

Guilt

During this time, I was tortured by the question of my own guilt. Is my (taxing) personality the reason for my isolation? Am I not conforming enough? In addition to my problems and sleepless nights I get these negative feelings that it is my own guilt that causes me to be isolated and I could not break away from these thoughts. Sometimes I did not speak to an adult for up to 10 days. Loving my son unconditionally – but not able to offer him a father, grandmother, sisters or friends or aunties – broke my heart more than one time.

On X-Mas and his first birthday we celebrated all alone. I was willing to celebrate the festivities and I never felt that lonely in my life before.

Saved!

A well-organized daily routine really helped me to stay stable. Every evening and two hours before I fell asleep, I turned off everything: my doorbell, the mobile phone, and the internet. I ate breakfast every day at the same time and took care to eat and drink enough to avoid dehydration or hypoglycemia. I used to take homeopathic lavender pills. The knowledge of understanding this is just a phase of my life (deep in my belly, not only spoken thoughts in my head) and the luck to find a great day mother at my son´s age of one.

The daycare took care of my son from Monday through Friday, five hours a day.

This helped me recover as an individual. I´m not only a mother.

Big thanks and love to Alex and Dwayne. Alex took care of my son once a week for an hour, so I was able to see a therapist. Alex took care of her own boy who was the same age as my son. And thanks to Dwayne who offered me Thai Massage in exchange for dinner.

This help was priceless.

After I made it through the worst time in my life, I started thinking about my new realities as a single mom.

Gentrification

Berlin is a place that has been discovered by capitalism slowly after the separation of East and West Berlin. The the sale of the city are on it´s way, but not finished yet. This change starts limiting my possibilities of participation. Everything became more expensive and the public life I can afford became smaller for me. And it brings another class of people to my hood; the petty bourgeois.

I´m a tattooed mother of a black kid. Although we are living in a multicultural part of Berlin, the prejudice won´t cease.

At the same time, parenting styles have changed a lot in 17 years (the age of my oldest). The theories about the mother's role in the last century have changed a lot. I´m a strict mom which is often interpreted as a less loving one. While I give space to my child to explore on his own, it gets interpreted as "she doesn't care."

But however you act as a mother, it seems like you can only fail.

At least I take care of my own needs.

Sexuality

I feel my own desires to act out sexuality, to talk about it, and to claim it is a political act, not a private act.

But I also ask myself how to protect my child from my own sexuality. We live in a small flat and I don´t want my child to see different partners.

I ask myself how my boy will grow up and handle this. A sexual single mother. As if my sex life is going to change in a small flat where you can hear everything.

At the moment, my boy is still little and I date on my kitchen table when he´s in bed.

I enjoy sex, but because of missing sleep I can happily go without it as well.

Identification

After seven years of being single, I pine for any kind of relationship because I spend much time alone at home. I do not know what kind of relationship I want. With every partner I have different needs and I´m open to many options.

However, I´m not really in a place where I can open myself to another man.

I´m really thankful that my mother did not have multiple changing partners. She was enough for herself. She had her (bad paying) job, friends and lived a fulfilled life. Our (difficult) relationship wasn't disturbed by others. There were no highs that come with falling in love and no mourning when someone left. I experienced that at friends' houses and I know I don´t want my child to experience that coming and going of man I thought I loved.

For sure, this blocks me from being open-hearted. At the same time, I wish there was a black man by my side, someone who could give my son an identity. I´m afraid I am not enough identification for my own child. Me as a white woman and him as a black boy... that maybe he can´t see himself in me.

I want to be as strong as possible for my child.

The knowledge of patriarchal structures is helpful for me; it helps me to overcome my private problems.

I´m afraid sometimes that I will collapse in this life.

This feeling is in conflict with my desire to show my son the only important thing; the happiness of being alive.

At least: "I'm the universe my child needs."

Beginning
Liz Darling

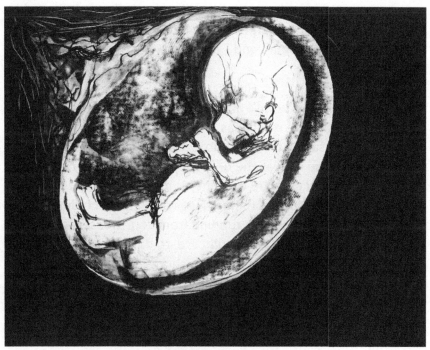

Conté on Plastic Paper.

Ripping out the Rotten Roots of Patriarchy

Irene Sanchez

I WALK INTO HIS OFFICE TO PLEAD. The prosecutor tells me when I am about to get up to leave that if he lets him off and doesn't do anything he is putting a target on my back. I want to tell him, Mr. Prosecutor, I am a woman and I was born with a target on my back.

I think back to how it wasn't all about my son's father, my son's father who was the reason I was in this office pleading with the prosecutor, not saying he didn't do it. Did he assault me? Yes. I was there because he was the only support I had for my son. To think my son could grow up without his dad and that my whole life could collapse, but the thing is I was also barely holding it together. I was a single mom running from courthouses for a separate stalking case, this assault case, to daycare, to work, to do my research on my dissertation to finish my Ph.D. and back to daycare wondering how would I survive. How am I still here?

I think back to before these most recent years to before I had my son. I think about my ex-husband, my high school sweetheart who cheated on me. I think where did I learn my first lessons on misogyny and patriarchy? We learn them young. We learn that it is normal. We learn this is how you get and keep a man. We learn obedience. We learn obedience willingly or have it unwillingly forced upon us through abuse. I was told at a young age, I wanted to do what I wanted to do as if it were a bad thing and that I didn't know when to be quiet. I learned at a young age, we don't even own the right to our bodies, to say no and feel safe. They had taken innocence from us at a young age. We learn patriarchy through speaking and by speaking we also learn that there is a consequence to speaking up or speaking out. For many of us this happens in the home and if this oppression happens there first, this is also our first battleground and where we must fight against it in order to win. We are at war. Our homes are the battlegrounds and too many of us have been causalities.

I remember back to when I got divorced to that high school sweetheart, how I was asked by family if he had hit me, as if that would be the only acceptable excuse for getting divorced, but the thing is he didn't and I wanted to pursue my goals. Then there came a time when men did hit me and I stayed. I stayed for fear. For threats my son would be taken from me and I kept rising and fighting every single day for him and myself.

I think back to those days and wondered how I even survived. I returned to my hometown with new battles that were really old ones. My son watching me now, reminding me how he remembers when he sees men treat me poorly or when I see women also reinforcing patriarchal behaviors. I realize I will have to fight patriarchy the rest of my life. I am raising a son who I want to know this is not the way it should be. I am a single mother on welfare. We came back to no stable housing and very little financial and emotional support. It is a vulnerable position to be in, but that doesn't mean I accept, submit, and stay silent. I think to myself what kind of system allows this to continue happening. It is not only patriarchy; it is a system that dehumanizes women and particularly women of color and our labor. It is a system that tells us we are not enough, that we are wrong, that we need to be silent when what we really need to do is speak, write, yell, dance and sing. Patriarchy kills, but as a single mother I have learned silence has killed far too many of us already. My son is watching and I have had enough. Ya Basta.

Single Mom: Sometimes Duel, Sometimes Duet

Veronica Cioaric

I WAS BORN AND RAISED and still live in an ex-USSR country. A small, corrupted and poor country. A country where if you are not married before age 25, people start making fun of you. A country were men rule everything, and you HAVE to obey.

A country where a male pharmacist made sexist jokes if you, as a woman, bought condoms or urgent contraception pills. A country where a female driver is considered a stupid blond who slept with the driving teacher to pay for her license.

A country where 20% of female students drop out of school because they have babies. A male student with a child is never forced to stay home with it – the wife does. I was 18 when I got pregnant. Not because I was not informed or too stupid at the time. It was an accident, and I preferred to give birth instead of getting an abortion.

I married the guy and we divorced six years later. And there I was, with no proper job because I kept going to university with every little bit of strength I had. No house of my own. No car. With everyone blaming me and hating me. "How could you? He's the father of your child! You should bear everything! He brings bread to the table, you should have been grateful!"

Well, I was not.

The last three years of the marriage were a nightmare for both of us. We hated each other and used to fight all the time. I had to move back to my parent's home, to the room I grew up in. I had to face them every day, and those looks they gave me... and my child asking me all the time: "Where's my dad?" I had to have two jobs, ask my mother to stay with my child, and deal with her calling me six times a day complaining about my bad lifestyle, about my bad choices, about how little money I made and how my son was misbehaving. I had to come home after 12-14 hours of work, cook for my child, bathe him, do lessons with him and... tell him stories, read, laugh, answer billions of questions and, again and again, make up lies why his father said he would come over but he didn't. Why didn't his dad call, why why why...?

It was much harder because of my son's asthma. Other parents will understand this. Constant cough for weeks, fever, projectile vomiting and sleepless nights. I was carrying him around the house and singing to him so he could rest. I wished I had someone to help me. I wished I had someone to tell me that everything was going to be okay. I wished I was stronger, maybe... my precious, sick and crying kid would finally fall asleep, and I'd walk around the house with him lying on my shoulder and silently cry. We were alone.

From some perspectives I was to blame. I divorced. I wanted to separate from his dad. I had to fight everything alone... bills, cooking, cleaning, laundry, homework, dish washing, 8-hour day job plus translation work or other projects at home... Going to my son's school, playing with him, talking to him, nursing him through his asthma, staying in hospitals with him, buying him clothes, shoes, medicine, toys, books.

I had to cope with my intimate life too. I had to keep my son away from the men I sometimes dated. I did not want him to get hurt again... to feel abandoned, again... to be disappointed, again. I had to fight with my mom all the time: "What kind of mother are you?

You spend your whole day at work, instead of being with your child?!" Yes, yes I did – and still do work a full day. Nobody else is paying my bills.

You know what makes me still smile? That time is on my side. Every day, my son grows stronger, older, wiser, closer to me. We are a team now. He is 13. I earn more money now. We go out and laugh a lot and fight over dirty shoes. But I feel free now. And life is not as hard as it used to be. And I have someone to help me out.

Never be afraid to claim your freedom. Never be scared to be alone. A tough peace is better than a silent war.

My Daughter Came Home Bruised

Kali Sunna

MY EX-HUSBAND has been on a cycle of abusing female family members for the entirety of the 16 years I have been involved with him. It seems to peak about every two years or so, with the usual emotional and mental abuse culminating in an episode of physical abuse.

In March of this year, after a visit with him, my daughter came back to me with a bruised and puffy upper lip and face, and cuts on her extremities. He had been at it again.

For about ten years, I have regularly notified Bedford County and Roanoke County officials of this man's episodes of violence and family abuse. Six years ago, Bedford Domestic Violence Services already had a file for our family that was two inches thick. At this point, I'm sure it's twice that. I have worked over the years on developing the strength to begin talking about our family experiences, to go to authorities for help, and I have obeyed VA law to act as a mandated reporter on family abuse.

However, regardless of this documented history of drama and abusiveness, officials seem surprised at each new episode of violence. They also decide that they won't look at the last time it happened or connect the dots – citing "it's in the past" as their reasoning. Each time, this man is able to convince authorities to act on his behalf, rather than on behalf of his victims. He doesn't do this alone; Bedford and Roanoke area officials are almost too willing to automatically disbelieve me and my daughter, as if they are acting from an itchy bias beneath their skin that is begging for an excuse to be scratched.

In the past, he's been quite successful at actually convincing the victims themselves, and others close to our family, that his outbursts were not his fault, and that his actions were not his responsibility alone.

This past March, when our child came home injured, I called her doctor right away. This is what any responsible parent would do. Her doctor instructed me to bring her to the ER, and the ER called both Bedford County CPS and the Bedford County Sheriff's Office. I shared texts with them that the child had sent me (while I was asleep) during the assault:

> "Dad won't leave me alone"
> "He's yelling at me"
> "He's making me cry"
> "Dad's screaming at me"
> "Mommy"
> "Mommy"
> "Mom"
> "Save me"
> "Help"
> "Now"
> picture of bloody hand
> "Pick me up at the school"
> (I ask what happened)
> "Dad"

My daughter explained to me, to a doctor in the ER, and to a Bedford County Sheriff's deputy that she had been called ugly, and "a fucking retard"; that she had been choked by her father's forearm, chased after, hit in the mouth twice causing a purplish swelling on her upper lip, picked up, dropped and dragged when she tried running for help, and banished to a couch in the garage for the night by herself with no heat in early March.

The buildup to the assault included open humiliation of a child about her changing body followed by a forceful lecture. The two adults were making degrading remarks about her developing chest from puberty; she was told that her chest was "ugly" and "nobody wants to see that" (the shape of her boobs underneath her shirt, which fully covered her). Lectures and punishments continued, and escalated from emotional abuse into physical abuse. When she tried to run to two different neighbor's houses for help, the physical abuse and following neglect was compounded. She was then left alone in an unheated garage all night in anguish with a purple swollen mouth, and not allowed to call me.

CPS was already familiar with our case and requested that I immediately go to the Court to request a protective order for the child. The worker specified that she would usually do this, but her caseload was heavier than usual at the time and she wanted the protective order to go into effect earlier than she could get to it – so it fell on me to go get it before the next visitation. Although they at first referred me to a different jurisdiction, the Court granted the protective order and set a date for a hearing.

Two hearings and several interactions with various officials have followed over the next several months. This was an enormous emotional burden for me and my daughter, and I will summarize as follows:

The deputy from the sheriff's office told me that her injuries were not severe enough for the Bedford County Sheriff's Office to press charges, but advised that I go to the Bedford County Magistrate and do so myself. When I followed up on his advisement and went, the magistrate's comment to me was, word for word, "What I see here is a parent trying to manipulate the system." She stated that she did not issue protective orders for juveniles, and she would not change a judge's custody order at the request of a parent, regardless of ER records showing injury after visitation. CPS waited for the Sheriff's Office to send a warrant before taking any action, which the deputy declined to do; so no action was taken by CPS.

At court in Bedford County J&DR, my ex-husband's story and his new wife's story were significantly different in details, which proved to me that they were just stories and lies being made up. I already believed my daughter, but this was further confirmation. My ex-husband's main tactic was to convince all those involved that the child's injuries came from her throwing herself on the ground and hurting herself. He had no explanation for her puffy, bruised upper lip.

Before the child came forward to chambers to testify, the Judge was notified that she has a past medical diagnosis of PTSD due to domestic violence, and was currently in a trigger due to new domestic violence, and needed to be handled with care. The Judge then proceeded to verbally attack and berate the child when she began to bravely give testimony in chambers. His attack was so mentally damaging to her that she could not sleep at night again until sometime in August later on in the year. After coming out of the Judge's chambers, she was horrified, choking on her own words, sobbing, trembling all over, and in a panic as she explained to me what happened to her.

The Judge had cut her off as soon as she started talking, told her to stop playing games with him, and said that her eyes and tears weren't going to get him. The Judge called her names, i.e. spoiled, and told her that what happened was her fault.

When she insisted that her father had choked her during visitation, the Judge intimidated her into silence by threatening her with "a jail cell."

She panicked for weeks and didn't sleep well for six months. As a result of this dishonorable conduct of a Judge toward a witness, her PTSD symptoms worsened significantly, but yet she would not be allowed unbiased mental health care.

Because I sent a cell phone with the child to her visitation, the Judge declared in an official order that I was "actively undermining the father's discipline." This was in opposition to testimony (by my ex-husband's new wife) that I encouraged the child over the phone to actively listen and cooperate with both her father and with his wife, just before the incident.

The GAL (Guardian ad litem) for the child told the court that the problem was with the child's behavior, not the father's. My response to this is that the father has been guilty of this behavior with other people since well before she was even born. Saying the responsibility for this lies with the child is fool-headed, shortsighted and has no basis or evidence. Manipulative abusers are well suited to convincing others to blame their victims for their drama, and it happens like clockwork every time this situation comes back around. This man used to swing his fist at my face repeatedly when I was pregnant and say that it was my fault and I was the one making him do it. It is just the typical mindset of abusers, and the GAL and Judge played right into it.

The GAL entered a CHIPS petition, which basically says the child is in need of services for alleged behavioral issues, and the Judge granted it. So now, CPS, therapists, and two court jurisdictions are focused on what must be fundamentally wrong with this child, rather than seeing the pattern of abusiveness and drama that has followed in the wake of the father with all kinds of different people for the last 16 years and focusing on that instead, which is the real problem.

Although I was home asleep at the time of the crimes, and although the Judge admitted temper problems with the father, much of the focus of the Judge's biased comments on the attachments to the court orders was on me.

Although physical injuries on the child were documented by the ER immediately after visitation with the father, the Judge actually accused me in writing of having fabricated the trauma presentation in the child. This also cannot logically be reconciled with the fact that this child already had a medical diagnosis of PTSD from trauma before this.

The Judge accused me of lacking the ability to co-parent, as if that had anything to do with what happened at someone else's house while I was sleeping at home alone in my own house.

The Judge excused the father's domestic violence as quote unquote "an overreaction by the father" and then, after verbally stating that the father "lost his cool," the Judge blamed the child for her own assault, in writing, in the attachment to the court order. The Judge actually took the liberty of diagnosing the child with a specific mental disorder which she has never been diagnosed with by her professional therapists.

The father was granted the authority to hand-pick a counselor, who was ordered to re-integrate the child back into visitation with him – regardless of their professional assessment of risk to the child. In this counseling process, the child refused to see her father again, and also notified the counselor that the father had terrorized her with a machete during visitation. Still, nothing was done to advocate for the child; her protective order was dissolved.

The child was ordered to undergo an invasive psychological evaluation, which is currently being scheduled by Roanoke County Social Services. The father faced no consequences. The case is ongoing and we live every day with the weight of this uncertainty and the resulting emotional pain.

In summary, a known abuser has struck and choked a child, causing facial bruising; called her names; dragged and dropped her through woods and brush when she tried to run for help, causing cuts and abrasions; terrorized her with a machete; gaslighted and lied and manipulated; and the Judge's way of handling it has been to threaten the 11 year old victim with jail and order ongoing invasive tests of her mental state to try to pin the blame on anyone but the man who did all of this, while attacking her mother as well. What happened in Court was psychological assault. It has taken months of intense support and love to help this child try to recover from her experience.

Judges hold immense power over children's lives, and should never be on the war path as this one was. In order to recover from trauma, child victims need to be heard and believed, and above all, they need to never be blamed.

I Want Ten Children

Martina Robles Gallegos

We'd been dating for a few years,
but neither one mentioned marriage.
The only ones interested in a wedding
were his sisters and brother-in-law.
His dad, of course, wanted a Vietnamese
daughter-in-law. I am Mexican
but too 'America' for the old fart.
I was in no hurry to marry yet;
I needed to finish college and get a job.
After I'd finished college and gotten a job,
my boyfriend's insecurities surfaced;
he feared I'd 'dump' him after achieving my goals.
I told him it was ok to get married now.
I felt I could take better care of myself
and family if I needed to.
The guy was as happy as a baby with a new toy.
We agreed to have a simple, private wedding.
My best friend and her husband went with us to Vegas.
On the way there we saw twisters, hail, and storms;
I should've listened to the signs.
My husband-to-be had a meltdown the day we were to marry.
I can't understand why I went through with it, but we did.
Four of us went to Vegas but came back five!
I knew immediately I'd gotten pregnant.
Two weeks later, all the signs were there.
I confirmed the pregnancy with home pregnancy test.
He was the first man I'd been intimate with,

but when I told him about my pregnancy, his response was,
"It's not mine. We don't even have sex."
Had I been somebody else, I'd have killed the bastard!
It was since then I knew I'd be on my own.
Before our baby was born, he'd said
he wanted ten children.
Needless to say, the previous relationship lasted more
than the marriage.
I even ended up in a Women's Shelter, going from bad to worse!
The damn place was so cold my baby almost got pneumonia.
I filed for divorce while at the shelter, but I still commuted to
work,
driving over forty-five minutes before the break of dawn
to drop my baby off at the nanny's before work.
Unfortunately, like many women, I returned to my hell;
he told me his friend had suggested marriage therapy.
I'd been asking for that for us for a long time.
I told him to go to hell.
I found and rented a room, always finding my situation worse than
before.
Eventually I bought a home for baby and me.
We'd agree on a child support amount, peanuts, really.
He never followed through. I filed for child support.
He never showed up to mediation or hearings.
He didn't comply with court-ordered child support.
Court garnished his wages; the result was the same; he left the
state.
D. A. Collected passport and driver's license;
he made the only visit to lie to judges and got his papers back.
He made about two more peanut-size payments
never to be heard from again.

Years later I suffered a ruptured Achilles' tendon,
followed by surgery, followed by massive stroke, coma,
brain and heart surgeries, and the loss of my dad;
my daughter was barely 15 at the time.
I let her dad know what had happened and to
be there for our daughter;
the bastard never even called her.
Now she's going to college and needs his financial support.
Again, he missed court hearings and isn't complying
with court-ordered back child support.
My daughter has made it clear she doesn't want anything
to do with him if he doesn't help her with college.
When my daughter graduated from high school,
I graduated from graduate school
since I resumed a Master's degree after my stroke.
He wanted ten children and couldn't take care of one,
but now he has a new and Vietnamese wife and two more
children.
I feel sorry for all of them; he'll destroy them sooner than later.

How Having a Child Changed My Life
Destiny Eve Pifer

SINCE CHILDHOOD I wanted to be a mom someday. I had envisioned my future with a husband, two kids, a nice house and a dog. Though it may sound cliché I also pictured a white picket fence. I had plans of holding on to my virginity until marriage but once I got in my twenties I began to feel peer pressure from my friends to lose it – and lose it I did to an unstable man whom I ended up having to put a restraining order on.

I had a pregnancy scare and had to get tested for STDs but still I threw myself in one relationship after another until I met a gorgeous man named Anton. Anton resembled one of those guys you would see on the cover of a romance novel. He was a hot Italian man who all the girls drooled over and he pursued me. I jumped into the relationship never asking questions and never researching his background.

From the very beginning of our relationship there were many red flags. For example, on our first date he brought along a man he introduced as his cousin. He claimed his cousin had just flown in from Italy. I naively believed both of them. While his cousin began pursuing my mother (who was fighting cancer) I was getting more deeply involved with Anton.

Before I knew it, I was having a passionate love affair and believing everything he told me, which was that he was an engineer and that the strange name that kept popping up on my caller ID was his boss. When Anton and his cousin Tony talked us into moving 50 miles from home we did.

Desperate to leave the projects where we lived, we traveled to a town rich in history but found ourselves living above a pizza shop in a small apartment. The moment we moved in, Anton mysteriously vanished claiming to be on an assignment. For months I didn't hear from him until he showed up at my door with a suitcase handcuffed to his wrist.

Once again, we started up our relationship but something had changed between us. There was no longer a spark. Instead he would visit me and take me out to dinner and then a quick roll in the hay. The whole time his phone kept going off with a text every ten minutes. He told me it was his boss. Meanwhile, Tony and my mother got married and she was dealing with a husband who claimed to work 12 hour days.

When I got pregnant, Anton was furious and tried to force me to get an abortion until I stood my ground and told him no. He once again vanished until our son was born. When I was pressured by the welfare office into filing for child support, Anton was even more furious. I found out from the child support services office that the name Anton provided was really an alias.

I began to secretly work with child support services and was stunned when I found out that "Anton" was married with four children. I was even more stunned to learn that he had no job and that he was possibly involved in drug trafficking. When Anton learned that I had him investigated he flew into a rage and began twisting my arm. When he pulled out a gun and threatened to kill me, I knew I had to get away from him. I turned to the local women's shelter and filed a PFA.

However, Anton was prepared with a ruthless lawyer by his side. Before I knew it I was being dragged into court and Anton was threatening to take our son and sell him in the black market. I once again stood my ground and fought back.

Finally, he agreed to let me have all parental rights and to move our son back to my hometown. But Anton wasn't done with his evil deeds. He had Tony file a PFA on not only my mother and brother, but on me.

Tony then revealed that he only married my mother to get into the country. I would also learn that Anton and Tony were lovers who had planned the whole thing. After fighting in court once again, I took my son, mom and brother and fled back to my hometown. I never heard from Anton again and Tony eventually divorced my mother. I don't get very much in child support but I don't care about that. All I care about is that he is out of my life for good.

It's been eight years since I have dated and the scars I carry from that relationship still remain. I fought hard to stop my evil ex from winning. Though I haven't dated anyone I have decided that I will not date until my wounds have healed, and most importantly, I have to find someone who will get along with my son who is now eight.

I have learned that when you become a parent you have to put someone else first. Having my son not only changed my life but it kept me from becoming more and more involved with the dangerous man that is his father.

My Very Own Mother's Day Proclamation

Brenna Jean Richart

I SOBBED FOR THE FIRST TIME in six months today. Throat aching loud, heaving sobs that come when someone dies. The kind that make you feel like you've been hit by a truck, then cement has been poured on top of you. It leaves you puffy-eyed and when you get up from the fetal position, there is a puddle of drool melting beautifully into your pillow, as your head pounds and your body aches.

Tomorrow is Mother's Day.

Mother's Day started as a day of Peace. "Many middle-class women in the 19th century believed that they bore a special responsibility as actual or potential mothers to care for the casualties of society and to turn America into a more civilized nation. They played a leading role in the abolitionist movement to end slavery. In the following decades, they launched successful campaigns against lynching and consumer fraud and battled for improved working conditions for women and protection for children, public health services and social welfare assistance to the poor. To the activists, the connection between motherhood and the fight for social and economic justice seemed self-evident," writes Ruth Rosen, a professor at UC Davis.

On the radio, I heard a DJ asking someone what they were going to do for their mother this weekend, "Take her to brunch," they responded.

I really hate brunch.

Mother's Day today is a day to honor your mother. One day to say thank you for all the bullshit she went through to make sure you were fed, clothed, smiling, and alive. One day to say thank you for a lifetime of sacrifice, a lifetime of lessons taught and learned. A lifetime of little moments that melted her heart, as well as feeling burned and alone.

My son and I were walking to the park, talking. I told him that our dinner plans had been cancelled earlier this week. He said, "They cancel a lot. Am I ever going to hang out with them?" I responded with, "Well, these things happen, sometimes people are really busy, or something comes up in their life." Lucas pondered that and said, "Is that just how things are, Mom?" A gust of wind blew hair into my face, and I felt stricken by his words. *Is this how things are?... Surely not everywhere.* I told him when people live in big cities, they have busy lives.

This conversation has been playing over and over again in my head. His reaction was so completely on point. He was disappointed and sad. He felt like he had been lied to. When people cancel plans on me, I just shrug and move on — it often has little effect on me.

Yet, I couldn't stop replaying this conversation — feeling devastated by my son's reaction. I wonder what it would be like if every time someone made a seemingly small decision, they had to answer to a seven-year-old who feels everything and states it openly. How different we would all behave if we had a tiny shadow following us around, saying, "That hurts my feelings," or "Why did you do that?"

As a mother I make all of my decisions with my son's face in mind. I think of how it will impact him now, and how it might impact him in two years, four years, or forty years. I think of my therapy sessions, how my first childhood memory is being told I had to go to school in my pajamas, crying as I tried to brush my hair with my fingers – terrified when someone else's mother took pity on me, and braided my hair. My first childhood memory is sparked by feelings of shame and fear. I look back now, and think of how frustrated and done my mother must have felt. How she probably was running late for work, and she had four other kids besides me to take care of, all while doing it alone. I think of how it can't have been easy for her.

Two years ago around Mother's Day, I was sitting in my English class as my teacher read "A Mother's Day Proclamation," written by Julia Ward Howe in 1870. Mother's Day originally started after the Civil War, as a protest to the carnage of that war, by women who had lost their sons.

She wrote, "Our husbands shall not come to us reeking with carnage... Our sons shall not be taken from us to unlearn all that we have been able to teach them of charity, mercy and patience. We women of one country will be too tender of those of another country to allow our sons to be trained to injure theirs."

As we read this poem I looked around at my classmates, they seemed unaware of the mothers in the room – me, fuming at the words; the other mother, sitting in front of me, shaking as she tried to hold back her tears. I wanted so badly to reach out to her, to hug her and hold her. In addition, I wanted to scream at my other classmates for not being more in-tune, for not understanding. I had read a paper of hers, this other mother – she had two sons and one of them died when he was seventeen years old, just a year before.

I really hate today's Mother's Day.

"In 1913, Congress declared the second Sunday in May to be Mother's Day. By then, the growing consumer culture had successfully redefined women as consumers for their families. Politicians and businessmen eagerly embraced the idea of celebrating the private sacrifices made by individual mothers. The industry's trade journal, bluntly put it, 'This was a holiday that could be exploited.'"

The personal is political. The maternal is political. My story is your story.

I was talking to another mom this week about racism, sexism, oppression, motherhood, life. She told me that Bainbridge Island, where she lives, is made up of 91% white people. She is a woman of color, a mother of two, with a family on the island. She is a full time student – working to get her degree. What with her three-hour commute, her family responsibilities and her school work, she doesn't have time left over to get involved with her community on Bainbridge – which isn't to say she doesn't want to.

She posted a question aimed at her community online, "Are we okay with the fact that Bainbridge is 91% white?" Many people responded to this and there was a discussion sparked about having low income housing on the island. She shared one comment with me that really stirred her up.

"My response is, you make choices in life, I'm glad she's going to college, but having children is a life choice. In an ideal world, you go to college, get a degree, get married, get established, then have children. Once you have children, *it is your responsibility to raise them as best you can*. It is not my responsibility to provide low income housing so you can live on Bainbridge Island. The cold hard facts are households with single moms have less upward mobility and a lot of them live on the poverty line. My advice is to hit the books, put your nose to the grindstone and maybe someday you can buy on Bainbridge." – As if that's all it takes.

Mothers feel the weight of the world in every interaction and conversation we have. We walk around feeling like we aren't doing enough, guilty that we have to explain to our kids, we can't do this or that, because mommy's too tired, mommy's too broke, mommy's too sick. Guilty that we are depressed. Guilty that we are in school, or at work, or just plain fed up. When we talk to each other, we feel this weight lifted just by knowing there are others out there like us, barely staying above water.

Another mama friend of mine burst into tears earlier this week. She hadn't gotten a lot of sleep because she stayed up doing homework and graphic design work for a grassroots organization that helps low income folks get food. She doesn't get paid for either job, yet she does it anyway. "It's not fair," She told me, as I hugged her and replied that her feelings are valid.

Our feelings are valid.

We feel so strongly that we need to help build better communities, create change for all people because we wipe the snot from our children's faces each day, and we want more for them. We sing them songs at night when we are exhausted and worn down, yet we still manage to make them smile. We understand pain in a way that is so deep, we can't even put it into words.

So many mothers aren't getting the support they need all year long. They have family that overlook them, never call, or write. They can't afford the luxury of having a car, or a day off.

They are judged by the way they look, dress, or act. By the job they have or don't have. Their kids are being picked up late, they are missing school or sports or homework due to lack of support, lack of community, lack of accountability by other humans in their lives.

Our children will be running the world someday. Do we really want them to grow up thinking mothers are in it alone? Do you want to be the person who taught a child the lesson that people disappoint, bail, or simply don't care, because they are not your responsibility? Children matter, yet mothers are the only ones who advocate for them, who feel tied to them, and who fight for them.

Mother's Day started as a Mother's Day for Peace. "Mother's Day wasn't always like this. The women who conceived Mother's Day would be bewildered by the ubiquitous ads that hound us to find that 'perfect gift for Mom.' They would expect women to be marching in the streets, not eating with their families in restaurants. This is because Mother's Day began as a holiday that commemorated women's public activism, not as a celebration of a mother's devotion to her family," Rosen writes.

There are more ways than brunch or a bouquet of dead flowers to show a mom you care. Honor a mother every other day of the year. Cook a meal when she really needs the support. Tell her you appreciate all she does for her kids. Read her children a book or take them to the library. Help a mother weed her garden or shovel her walk. Babysit. Take her children to the park. Pick up her kids from school. Be there for a mother and her children 365 days out of the year.

Nineteenth century women had it right when they spent thirty years devoted to bringing mamas of all walks of life together, to create peace for the world community.

Our capitalist, consumerist, patriarchal Mother's Day was created for you by corporations who want your money. They don't care about mothers, their children, or their sacrifices. Turn off your radio, skip brunch, and stop being part of the problem.

I'm Thinking

Lennée Reid

I am thinking about becoming a lesbian
As a self defense mechanism
Protecting my kid from being molested
Or me being beaten again
I'm thinking about trusting statistics
And not becoming one by building
A permanent wall protecting me from predators
Except except I don't know how
I see beautiful kind sweet women and I think
We could communicate with each other
Maybe she's a good cuddler
I wonder if she'll like my cooking
I am thinking about becoming a lesbian
Give myself a new life
To resurrect all those times I was bi
Live a life where I don't just remember
She tasted like candy
Multiply those experiences in to a relationship
With more depth and complexity than a threesome
I am thinking being gay would be a great way
To tell guys to go fuck them selves
When they lick their lips and say
My eight year old walks with a switch in her hips
Just like her mama
I am thinking of becoming a new me
I am thinking of letting myself free
Yeah maybe I'll try being a lesbian

Motherhood on Trial

Jakki McIntosh

I WAS SOUGHT OUT by a man six years older than me at the tender age of 16. As he pursued a close friend of mine at the age of 17, he patiently waited until I turned 18. We got together one time only which was a very traumatic experience. In short he raped me. I was very vocal about withdrawing my consent yet he did not honor that request.

At the age of 30 I am just now coming to terms with the severity of the situation and how I'll never get the proper justice for what he's done to me. He met our daughter three years after her birth and has used his male privilege, financial status to shame me as a woman and mother. His lack of respect for me is the same as the time he raped me. I am currently in the middle of a custody battle.

This happened in retaliation to me demanding child support as he does not properly support her. He then took to the law to legally harass me through his lawyer by requesting sole custody to evade paying child support. He used my financial status, his money, his male privilege to make me out as a bad mother. Countless frivolous motions... I struggle with the stress of caring for my children, having to suppress my feelings, and dealing with the harassment while constantly being scrutinized, demonized, and held to an unrealistic standard simply because I'm a woman.

The Life I Was Born to Live?

A.L.Hayes

APPARENTLY WOMEN MARRY THEIR FATHERS, but in my case that couldn't be further from the truth. As a child, I idolised my Dad and he could do no wrong. From the perspective of womanhood, I know that originally he was a man of his time. He went out to work, while my mother stayed home and looked after the children. My Dad earned the money, so he had control of the purse strings. He never left my mother short of anything, we had everything we needed and a lot more besides. My Dad didn't go to the pub after work and fall up the roads so out of his mind that he didn't even recognise his own children, which was a regular occurrence for many of our male neighbours. However, my mother never had any money of her own, except for the children's allowance, so she largely relied on him to provide for everything.

When my mother became ill, I suppose my Dad had to rethink his whole life. He was left to care for six children, look after a sick wife and hold down a full time job. He cooked, cleaned, did the washing and ironing, tasks that were not considered "men's work" back then. My Dad juggled everything, while instilling in us the importance of education. We grew up in what was considered an underprivileged area of Dublin—and given that we all did relatively well for ourselves and didn't end up in trouble with the police, is testament to the fact that my Dad was a Super Hero.

That's not a term I can use for my ex-husband. He came into my life about two years after my Dad died and I don't think I had got over that huge upheaval. I was lonely, I wanted somebody to love and I wanted to feel wanted. My ex appeared charming, had led an interesting life and was from a completely different cultural background than me. We were polar opposites and maybe that's what attracted me to him. The reasons why I undervalue myself could fill a psychology text book and are too numerous to go into here. Let's just say that my ex played on my vulnerabilities and could twist things around so that I ended up apologising for his misdemeanours.

When I met my ex I had a decent job, a brand new car, money in the bank and depression. Can I blame depression for the whole sorry episode that was our courtship and marriage? Not really. Maybe it played a part, but the reasons I stayed with him run much deeper than that. Time and again he would push me to the edge and when I felt I had reached breaking point he would reel me in again, telling me how much I meant to him. I chose to ignore all the times he had let me down, put me down and belittled me.

I went into the marriage with my eyes wide open, but my mind firmly closed. From the very start of our relationship, he took and took, but never gave anything in return. I worked full time and studied at night, but he would demean the jobs I had and say I only went to University for fun. All this from a man who couldn't hold down a job for more than five minutes. Yeah, it was great fun leaving the house at nine o'clock in the morning and arriving home near to midnight, only to find him stretched out on the settee, remote in hand, waiting for me to cook him something to eat.

His cultural background dictated that the housework was "women's work." It was the man's job to provide financially for his family, but I was the one shouldering both roles. To the outside world I maintained a front, pretending I was the self-assured person I used to be. Inside I felt like a fraud, putting up with

148

unjust crap, but burying my anger and resentment deep down so that I could have a quiet life at home. It's strange how the odd shove, slap or kick appears to become a normal part of a relationship. My ex would proclaim that it wasn't like he battered me.

Physical abuse can deliver a short, sharp, shock, but the scars from emotional abuse linger. The subtle put downs and humiliations, that friends and family wouldn't even notice, were like daggers in my heart. On our own he would berate me, calling me an alcoholic, a psycho and stating that all our problems were down to my hotheadedness. Despite all that, when I got pregnant we were both delighted. We had been married for about a year and a half and the previous Christmas had almost seen us split for good when he had pulled clumps of my hair out. I spent Christmas Day on my own crying my eyes out, but when he came back in the New Year, the story was all turned round and I was the culprit, not the victim. By that stage I was an emotional wreck and succumbed to his explanation.

Unfortunately, my first pregnancy ended in a miscarriage. We were both gutted and so were our families. He hugged me in the hospital when the doctor gave us the bad news and that is the last time I ever remember him being kind to me, or of feeling an emotional connection with him. I took time off from work to recover and only went back briefly, feeling that I couldn't cope. Of course his voice was inside my head encouraging me to give up work, as he was opening a shop and it was to his benefit that I worked there. Within months I was pregnant again and I was scared to death. I couldn't visualise my baby until I held him safely in my arms. At three months I started bleeding but thankfully it resolved itself and the pregnancy continued.

My ex never made any concession to my pregnancy or the worries and fears that besieged me. He would shove me out of bed in the mornings to go and open up his shop, while he slept on. It was easier for me to get up and go, than to argue with him. He wasn't prepared to put in the hard work associated with owning a business and so it was doomed to failure, only lasting about six months. When our son was born, we were broke. My family provided most of the necessities and I had my sick pay to fall back on. Depression hit me like a ton of bricks. My ex just sneered and told me I couldn't even look after my own child. I was exhausted both mentally and physically, and although I loved my baby I didn't get the chance to enjoy him. My whole life had changed, but my ex just carried on as normal, arsing around and visiting his mates.

When our son was 11 weeks old I went out to work in a women's refuge. Oh, the irony of it. I was dealing with women who were fleeing abusive situations, giving them advice on how best to deal with the court system, while living a similar nightmare at home. I did evening shifts and had to leave the baby with a sitter, as my ex had started working as a taxi driver. It was a slog, but I relished being independent once again and having a life outside the home. Then I became pregnant again with my daughter, which came as a bit of a shock.

I was so stressed out and tired during that pregnancy that I lost weight and suffered from recurring kidney infections which required me to be hospitalised a couple of times. Being left to look after our son didn't suit my ex at all. When I had to stay in for an extra night, he hurled abuse down the phone at me. The fact that a kidney infection during pregnancy can put the baby's life in danger, didn't matter one iota. Things came to a head on the Easter weekend when we had a row and he tried to hit me while I was holding our son. We split up.

Our daughter was born two weeks early and my sister and my niece got me through that day. My ex showed up hours after the birth with a bunch of flowers and a teddy bear. Being left on my own, in an isolated area, with two babies to look after was a nightmare. Depression visited again and at times I truly feared for my own sanity. A month after my daughter's birth my ex showed up in the middle of the night, more or less saying that if I didn't take him back he wouldn't see the kids again. I agreed to a reunion. I knew that I was making the biggest mistake of my life, but I suppose I felt some help would be better than none.

We struggled on for another year. He was taxiing most nights, sleeping during the day, and out with his friends on his night off, so I rarely saw him. I'm not saying he never changed a nappy or bottle fed one of the kids, but he only did it when he felt like it, not when I needed him to. The following summer we went on holiday to his home country for a family wedding and I remember looking at him during those two weeks, when we were forced to spend so much time together and thinking that I had no feelings for him whatsoever. Any love that had been there was long since gone and I didn't even have the energy to hate him.

Not long after we returned from that holiday he was ganged up on by a couple of thugs, who set his taxi on fire. He wasn't badly injured, but when he came home and told me the story I couldn't even find it in my heart to feel sorry for him. He was out of work again, so the big plans of starting his own business were once more resurrected and he borrowed money from the Credit Union, which was flittered away with nothing to show for it. The final split was caused by something totally inconsequential. While I spoke to a friend on the phone he was mithering me, asking me if I had nothing else to do and bugging me about clearing away some gardening tools I had been using before I'd taken the call. It was the straw that broke the camel's back and I just snapped.

151

Being left on your own with two toddlers is no easy thing, but peace of mind is priceless. Not having to listen to somebody else constantly put you down, not walking on eggshells in case you upset them, is so liberating. In those early years I made sure I fostered a relationship between the kids and their Dad, because I would never let it be said that I had stopped him seeing them. Sometimes now I wonder if I made the right decision, as I hate the fact that he has any influence over their lives. However, I chose him to be their father and I must live with my decisions as best I can.

Apart from the kids, the sum total of my marriage was a two bedroomed, run down old cottage with a mortgage and no maintenance from my ex. I changed the mortgage to an interest only payment, thinking that when things improved financially I would restart regular payments. When my kids were three and four years old, I went back to college to get a Degree in Psychology, reasoning that this would improve my chances of securing a higher paid job and thus provide a better standard of living for my little family. For three years I travelled for almost three hours a day during the week, looked after my kids, completed assignments and sat exams, while battling with an ever dwindling grant, that made it harder and harder to survive. Receiving an honours degree, I was very proud of my achievement, until reality struck and I realised I had the paperwork, but the country was now in the middle of a recession and there wasn't a job to be had.

The kids were getting too old to share a bedroom, so I had to give up my own room in order to accommodate them and found myself sleeping on a bed-settee in the sitting room. The cottage was cold and damp, impossible to heat and the septic tank overflowed whenever we had heavy rain. I had fought to hang onto our home when I separated because I didn't want to cause more upheaval for my kids, but now it had become a millstone around my neck. I began to hate it and eventually came to the decision that it was madness to throw good money after bad. It would be easier to hand the keys back to the bank and walk away. I had just come to terms with this course of action when I had a bad car crash.

The result of the crash was broken bones in my spine, broken ribs and a broken ankle. Even then my ex couldn't be relied upon to help out, so instead of going to rehab, like the doctors wanted me to do, I came home in a back brace and on crutches. The crutches only stayed with me for a few weeks, but the back brace was my constant companion for three months. Everyday tasks were a difficulty and if it wasn't for the help of a very good friend, I never would have managed. The reality of my isolated situation only hit me harder during those months and made me more determined than ever to leave the cottage and start a new life.

And now, two years later, I am finally piecing my life back together. Living near town I have a good circle of friends, who encourage and support me in so many ways. I love my children fiercely and they are the only reasons I don't regret my marriage. I'm currently doing a course that is helping me to see light at the end of the tunnel. Many moons ago I loved to paint and write, but I put those things into a box and shoved them into a dark corner of my mind, when I decided to be an adult. I am now discovering that those long ignored talents could be the key to my future. I may never be a millionaire, but every little success writes the story of who I was, who I am and who I want to be. Depression still snaps at my heels and occasionally catches my coattail, but I will never let it consume me.

Single Mother
LuLu

THERE IS NO SINGLE MOTHER, no one person who mothers us wholly and completely though we long for ours to do so. There are no single mothers who are utterly alone for there is a way to always be aligned with a perfect mother.

When I was 29, I received my doctoral degree and swiftly became a single mother. Teaching at UCLA gave me the courage to see the man that was my husband was a shred of a person. Our marriage was void of connection, and he lied to me. I was naïve and seduced by his Ivy League degree so I believed a lot. When he told me his alma mater invited him back for a fellowship, I believed him and hoped the new setting would be good for our marriage and family. We left our home, packed possessions into storage, and traveled across the country for the promise of: free on-campus housing, free childcare, free utilities, free medical insurance, and a modest annual salary. It sounded too good to be true, because it was. In couples therapy, I voiced my concern that we were about to leave our home and didn't know our new telephone number, address, medical insurance info, or anything for that matter. Our therapist, a well-respected academician herself, reassured me that this was common practice in academia.

In September 2002, we left our home for the other coast. With two boys ages two and three, the journey took two weeks with stops along the way to visit various cities in the US. When we arrived in our destination city, my husband suggested we look for a place to live. While it may seem like a simple suggestion, it caused great rage within me. I didn't understand why we would need to look for a place to live when we were assured on-campus housing as a benefit of his fellowship. I left him there, there in that city. Alone at the hotel. Packed our gorgeous boys into our SUV, and hauled off to the nearest city where I knew people.

Before I tell you what happened next, let me state: There never was a fellowship. I personally spoke with the professor my husband said was responsible for extending the fellowship who fully denied ever offering my husband a fellowship. The annual salary my husband quoted was the amount MBA graduates receive when they stay on for a fellowship. My husband had a masters degree, but not in business administration, nor was he a recent graduate transitioning into the fellowship program.

The nearest city where I knew people was the one I grew up in. People opened their homes, welcomed me, and within a few weeks, I was offered a job as a school psychologist. Our boys were enrolled in preschool at the local synagogue, and we were quickly getting situated. I was a good enough mother, even in crisis. My husband knew where we were; he came and visited us. He stayed with our boys when I went to meet a friend; then he had dinner with my brother afterwards. The very next day, when we were supposed to meet to discuss the terms of separation, he never came. Instead, a process server arrived with divorce papers, while police and social workers removed our sons from the preschool center.

My heart sunk. I still haven't processed the magnitude of that moment – even though it's been almost 15 years since it happened. My first husband set me up, pretended to be on good terms with me, and cooperating in the search for divorce terms, but he wasn't. He was establishing me as a mentally ill woman who was in a psychotic episode and kidnapped her kids to a foreign country. Back in our home state, he filed ex-parte documents stating that I had absconded with the children, without his knowledge. He called the psychiatrist who was prescribing an anti-depressant for postpartum depression to confirm for him that I was unstable. He told her that I had taken our kids to another country, and that he felt I was unstable. She said that would be plausible without even speaking with me. One week after learning this, I called her and asked her why she didn't pick up the phone and call me to see if I was OK. She took my husband's words as truth, and the courts in our home state took my kids away. My doctor treated me as mentally unstable without even contacting me, and upon the word of a man she never met.

We spent weeks in a Hague trial where the courts determined we needed to return to our home state to adjudicate the divorce. I lost my job, and returned to the city where my mother and her husband lived. They took me in, with my young sons. And, I quickly got a job as a psychologist at the largest special education non-profit in the US. After a custody evaluation, it was determined that I was the better parent, only by a little, and we split custody with me having 55% of the time with our boys. Within a couple of years, my ex-husband drifted away.

This is the part of the story where the single mother theme splits. Not only was I a single mother, but I was living in my mother's house with her husband. This is where I learned that my mother failed me, and tried to rescue me from the danger of those failures. It's where I began to notice that:

There is no single mother, no one person who mothers us wholly and completely though we long for ours to do so.

It is also where I learned once again that men think mothers who do things they don't like are mentally ill, and worthy of demonization.

One night, I was out at the hardware store with my then beloved, and now current husband of 13 years. After putting my boys to sleep in their grandmother's home, with her there, as well as her husband, I stepped out for a few hours. Upon my return, I learned that the boys had woken up while I was out. Though I trusted my mother and her husband to care for the boys should this happen, my step-father was triggered and enraged by the fact that I had failed my boys by being out when they woke up. He charged at me to attack, and my mother jumped in the way.

Upon reflection, I often thought my mother was being courageous in that moment; protecting me like the mother bear I wanted her to be. She wasn't. She was a party to the abuse that night because she allowed herself to be married to a man who did it to her for a decade. She welcomed her daughter and grandsons into a home she knew was dangerous. Long before the fellowship crisis with my husband, I had asked her to help me leave my marriage and raise my kids. She declined. And yet, there she was "ready to help" when the whole mess wound up in a Hague trial and I was homeless.

Her "readiness to help" was taken as maternal love, care, empathy, and compassion. Instead, it was a way of bringing me into the web of abuse she was in, rather than leaving it with my help and to help me too. On the night my sons awoke while I was out, we all fled at midnight when my step-father attacked me. There was no way I was living in a house where a man charged to attack me for being out when my boys woke up. And, my mother decided to come along with me.

The reason this story segues towards my mother is because she influenced the type of mother I saw myself as. Adrienne Rich wrote about matrophobia, the fear of becoming one's mother. I was never afraid of becoming the type of mother mine was (though in some ways I did;) I was committed to being a completely different kind of mother. Paula Caplan wrote, in *The New Don't Blame Mother*, that our culture raises mothers to unattainable ideals that lead to devaluation, demoralization, and powerlessness. Mothers are in an impossible bind with unrealistic expectations placed upon them concurrent with the myth of inferiority placed upon women.

Caplan (2000) wrote: "...most mothers are insecure about their performance as mothers and desperately need the approval of other women, including their daughters." The culture makes it hard for women to be good enough mothers. This combined with the two crises made it hard for me too, to see the good enough mother I was. While my mother may have needed my approval about the kind of mother she was, I couldn't give it to her. There were times, one long before the crises – and one just a few years ago, where my mother firmly planted herself on the side of my abusers who called me mentally ill. She confirmed it to my current husband just a few months ago when he dialed her number by accident. My self-perception as a mother was wrought with fear that I was mentally ill, and my mother played a critical role in those fears before and after other men had as well.

My mother reminds me of Madeleine Albright's words: "There is a special place in hell for women who don't help other women."

Beware of the woman who helps you see the worst part of you as the whole part.

To find the single mother within me, the one who is always aligned with a perfect mother, I had to accept that both my mother and I are well, only human. In her broken humanness, she exposed my sons and I to dangerous situations, which meant I needed to separate from her too. This separation would take 10 more years because of the intense bond between us, however it was essential to finding both the Goddess within me, and the Good Mother too. The Good Mother is the inner wise and wonderful part of me that always knows. She knew to hightail it to the city I grew up in when the fellowship crisis arose. It wasn't a mistake to go there, even though the courts called it kidnapping. It was where I found safe shelter for my kids and I, and a job when my husband lied to me and led us to be homeless. The Good Mother within me knew that community would ease this crisis. She knew that when a man charges at you, that place is no longer safe and it is time to leave. The Good Mother resides within me, and is always with me. She is Me.

The Good Mother is the part of me that I can turn to when I need nurturance. She is the part of me that knows just what I need when I need it. She always has perfect empathy, because it's Me giving myself self-empathy. Cultivating this part of myself required complete emancipation from my mother, but this isn't the story for all single mothers – just mine. It helped me find the Good Mother within, which in turn created a Good Mother for my kids.

It's been more than a decade since both these crises occurred. My ex-husband disappeared from our lives, leaving financial ruin and broken hearts of young fatherless men. Though my second husband has been a tonic for my soul, he hasn't been the same gift to my boys. His own mother and father impacted him, making it hard for him to find his inner Good Mother, and be the Good Father he desires. He is a good father and step-father; he just falls short of the kind he'd like to be.

There is no single mother, no one person who mothers us wholly and completely though we long for ours to do so. There are no single mothers who are utterly alone for there is a way to always be The Good Mother.

Shit Happens

Written and experienced by Shareen

WE MOVED TO SAN ANTONIO from a little town in West Texas, just the two of us – my little boy and me. He was two, and we were recently estranged from his father who tried forcibly to get into the back door. I had some friends with me and we were startled to hear the sound of someone trying to break into the apartment.

We lived with family for the next year and then in February of 2015, Odin was taken from me in the most horrible way. After waiting years for a hearing with the OAG and the judge, a Facebook post of mine was shown without context and the judge thought I was a drunk. I assure you, I don't have an alcohol problem – I will drink socially, but no issues. I cried from the pit of my soul out in the hallway filled with people, but I didn't care. My ex tried to say something to me, but I remember screaming at him, "do I look like I am prepared for a conversation with you right now?"

"I just..."

"No! Look at me. GET AWAY FROM ME!"

As he and his mocking comments sauntered away, I fell back into tears. Comforted by a nearby abuelita, I steadied myself and began to realize my world was changing.

The car seat was empty.
I didn't have to make dinner.

I didn't have anyone to bathe and sing songs with.

No one to dress or give his hair a comb.

Empty car seat again.

Had to work. Got to eat. Could barely function.

I passed on his toys and shoes to my dad who made sure they got to Odin.

Broken. Completely broken.

And then came a man... there's the beginning of the end. He was dark-skinned, built, and his smile was so entrancing. Delightful and giving, he liked to avoid dramatic situations. He seemed like a fit. At first. What I didn't realize was that I was looking for someone to love, because I lost the child who I loved and lived for constantly. A lonely home can break someone.

We were cute for a few months, then I guess he became bored with me, which is why things ended the way they did. The police mentioned there was some other pregnant woman who filed charges against him for cutting her or some craziness like that.

I found out when I filed assault charges – after a threat he made against me when dropping me at work that made me seriously worry – things had escalated at home and things only get worse. I also read a printout of his rap sheet. It revealed what I suspected all along – that he had been in trouble almost every year of his life.

By then, I was eight months pregnant. My coworker took me home and I didn't answer my ex's calls or texts. He also left voicemails saying that I was "putting everyone I knew in danger," but I didn't listen to them until months later.

The next morning, in an attempt to "rescue" my car, he saw me getting out of my friend's vehicle.

He was sitting in my car, apparently headed to my job to find me – and then he took off after us. I called 911 immediately and recorded a two-mile chase, down several major streets. He would speed up in front of us and shove on the brakes. He spun us out a couple times by colliding with the side of the bumper (PIT maneuver), and when he thought we were finally stalled out, he jumped out and tried punching my window to shatter it, screaming, "What did I do?!"

I'm just sitting there a screaming mess. He went back to the car at the same time my coworker got the car going. We took off – speeding and running red lights – and ended up at the substation. Even though I knew he hated cops, I knew he hated me more, and he would follow me if he could. I couldn't open my door from the crash, so I grabbed my shoes and my purse and ran – almost falling headlong, fully pregnant and unbalanced.

They let us in the back. My mom drove up from Corpus Christi, and I hid out there over the weekend until the police caught him. I talked to the arresting officer and asked him to put the handcuffs on a little tighter for me.

On December 21, 2015, Joy Victoria was born. Because we are Joyous in the help of the Lord, and Victorious because God has already won the war. I reconnected with Jesus (not Christianity) and studied him and his words. These gave me a new lease on life.

I was going to end it there, but what's important is this: *Shit happens*. What defines you as a person is how you handle what comes your way.

More Than Alright

Anonymous

I WAS 18 when I met my daughter's father. Matt was different than anyone I had met before and I was drawn to him. At 21, he lived a transient and parasitic lifestyle, unemployed and living in a self-declared "flop house" in an economically desolate Midwestern town.

He sold drugs, experimented with psychedelics, and drank heavily. Matt was unreligious, unlike me (despite my devoutness, I longed for the mental freedom to question religious authority). His lifestyle was a stark contrast to my sheltered and structured upper-middle class upbringing. I envied his freedom and his bohemian ideals, especially at a time when I was struggling to make life-defining choices as a college freshman.

We spent a lot of time exploring abandoned buildings, tagging underpasses, smoking pot, going to rock shows, watching obscure films, and navigating the town on foot. It felt, for the first time in my life, that I had something of my own. It was my late rebellion, after being a "good girl," held tight under my parents' thumb throughout my adolescence.

Our relationship was a tumultuous off-and-on train wreck. Matt was regularly verbally abusive and took advantage of me in every possible way. He convinced me to loan him almost $1000 (the rest of my whittled-down life savings by that time) in increments, promising to reimburse me when he got inheritance money from his father who had recently passed away.

Instead of paying me back, he broke up with me when he got the inheritance check. This was one of many times we would break up and get back together. He grew marijuana plants in our apartment, and facetiously threatened to slit my throat in my sleep if I got rid of them. I could never gauge how serious that threat was, but I didn't want to find out. Because the apartment was in my name, I was terrified of reporting him to the cops for fear that I would be prosecuted for growing too. Occasionally my landlord would knock on the door unannounced at 8 or 9 o'clock in the morning, and in a panic I would rush downstairs and let him know that yes, everything was fine with the apartment. In retrospect, he might have been checking on me, having sensed something was "off."

Matt cheated on me more than once, often with teenagers, which, at the tender age of 19, and in conjunction with a pornified pedophile culture, made me feel somehow "too old" to be sexually appealing. Instead of leaving him, as I obviously should have done, I somehow conflated my brainwashed sense of Christian "forgiveness" with "moving on," and tried to bury his transgressions and his utter disregard of my emotional, mental, financial, and physical safety.

A year later, after a rollercoaster of verbal and psychological abuse, Matt moved his things out for good. I thought the ordeal was finally over. I stopped paying for my birth control pills. The $20 / month cost seemed like an unnecessary expense. After all, my campus job only paid $5.15 an hour. I was nearly immobilized in my grief over losing him. My reasoning had become incredibly convoluted. Despite the way he treated me, I loved him and thought that what we had was irreplaceably unique. Having largely distanced myself from my well-meaning friends who told me over and over to leave the relationship, I felt like no one understood me except him.

166

Matt never left me alone to heal. He preyed on my vulnerability, finding ways to keep me in a kind of psychological limbo where he could always have me on his terms. He would knock on my door late at night, and I would let him in as a respite from my emptiness; the prodigal lover back for one more hour.

I found out that I was pregnant about two months after we broke up. We went around and around in circles arguing about what to do – should I get an abortion? Have the baby? Have it and give it up for adoption? "It" felt so abstract. Whatever I said, he wanted the opposite. It made him livid that he didn't legally get a say in the matter. HE wanted to be the one to make the decision. Once, when we were lying on the bed arguing, he jumped on top of me, grabbed me around the throat and started strangling me out of rage. I thought he was going to kill me. Another time, he threw me into a wall. I regretted even telling him that I was pregnant.

When my parents found out about my pregnancy, they were devastated. They acted like it was 1950, and I was a disgraceful harlot... As if being married (to a man, of course) would have somehow legitimized my right to be pregnant. I simply told them I was just going to have an abortion, and not to worry themselves about it, despite the fact that I hadn't made any plans to schedule anything, and I didn't have the money to go through with it anyhow. Opposed to abortion (and likely worried what conservative friends and members of our community would think if they found out) my parents insisted that I consider all the options before making a decision.

I visited a "crisis" pregnancy "Medical Clinic," where I talked to a kind Christian woman named Jennifer. They would not give me an abortion referral, however, as the "Clinic's" essential purpose was basically to convince young women to NOT have abortions. I was given a sonogram there, allowing me to hear the heartbeat. I went back to talk to Jennifer on many occasions. She was an understanding, nonjudgmental ear that I needed so badly. I also went to a Planned Parenthood clinic to talk to someone about the possibility of having the baby and giving it up for adoption. Through that interaction, I had a sense that the industry felt contrived and coercive, a way to funnel babies of economically disadvantaged women into largely heteronormative, two-parent, affluent, Christian homes. It felt like a brand of bullshit that I couldn't articulate at the time.

To attain an abortion, I would have had to drive for hours to the nearest clinic. I would have had to beg my friends for cash, or find someone willing to let me use their credit card. It's unlikely my insurance would have covered it at the time. My parents wouldn't have supported me in having an abortion. I was also afraid of physical retaliation from Matt if I made that choice. With all this weighing on me, it was much easier to find ways to justify "keeping the baby..." so I did.

As the years have passed, I've told myself and others that I became a single mother by choice. It's true to an extent. I had a baby, knowing full well that her father would be a deadbeat dad at best and a danger at worst.

Had I been desperate enough to end my pregnancy, maybe I could have persevered against the obstacles standing in my way... but the older I get, and the further I get away from it, I realize that my "choice" to become a mother wasn't as empowered as I would like to believe. Would I have gone through with my pregnancy had I not been afraid of my ex-boyfriend? Would I have been brave enough to go against my parents' wishes, had I not been financially dependent on them? Would I have even gotten pregnant in the first place if paying for birth control had not been a hardship? I am not trying to play the victim, as I was certainly complicit in my role, but these are legitimate factors that influenced the situation. I can't help but wonder how it would have played out in a part of the country where reproductive healthcare was affordable, easily attainable, and didn't come with the heavy stigma that it carries here in the Bible Belt.

Despite our ambivalent beginnings, my daughter is the love of my life. I have built my whole world around her. Motherhood has changed me in countless positive ways. However, it's hard not to wonder what it would have been like to have a baby with a true partner, someone I loved and who loved me, instead of this antagonist in the background who I feel a subtle, constant need to protect my child from. I may never know.

Matt has been a thorn in my side for the majority of my daughter's life. I've had to deal with his threats throughout the years, and his nearly constant harassment over not being satisfied with our custody/visitation order.

When my daughter was a toddler, I managed to get a temporary custody order that would grant him supervised visitations only, for a myriad of reasons. When he interacted with us during those early years, his focus was almost always more on me than it was on our daughter. He wanted to be under my skin; he wanted to know that he still had power over me. There have been many times throughout the years that he has shown irrationality, instability, and a scary sense of entitlement. Over the years I've played by the rules of our court order, all the while holding my breath that he will stay just far enough away to not pose a true threat. The temporary custody order eventually became a permanent custody order, and it is one of my deepest fears that he will take me back to court someday and we will have a judge who sympathizes with "men's rights," overlooking my daughter's safety.

Last year, Matt went to prison, and upon his release, he has been a little more distant, which has been like a wave of peace, despite the fact that my daughter is now at the age where she's starting to feel injustice over not having a "real" dad. He's a near-constant scratching in my head though, just peripheral enough to keep on my radar. He is a demon who latched on to me, a trial I have to endure until my daughter is grown. There is a paradox in wanting so badly to just hang on my daughter's childhood and enjoy it to the last drop – and simultaneously looking forward to her growing up, so I will finally be free of his presence.

Single motherhood – the only kind of motherhood I have ever known – has been a tremendous blessing and a thankless job. I have a memory of running into one of my old teachers when I was pretty far along in my pregnancy, and instead of being congratulated, he said something akin to "I'm sure you'll be alright... someday." That comment stuck with me for years as a reflection of the way society marginalizes female-headed families and deems them illegitimate, shameful, and in need of pity.

That rhetoric is disempowering nonsense. Beyond the situation with Matt, things have been more than "alright." Our lives are excellent and I feel blessed in many ways. I am a teacher at my daughter's school. We make art, play soccer, and take trips. I recently bought a house. We are not wealthy but we are by no means living in poverty. Child support would be helpful, but as you can imagine, we don't receive any. I could attempt to get child support through our state's Child Support Enforcement Services (they handled our case previously yet were never helpful in delivering results), but since Matt is not antagonizing us much at the moment, I don't want to rock the boat. Taking that action would provoke him and I'd rather just deal with any financial strain myself and be free from his harassment.

My hope for single mothers – all mothers – is that we may never question our divine right to feel complete in our role as mothers, regardless of the presence or absence of men in our lives. May we live in a world free from misogyny, male violence, patriarchal religious propaganda, and constant political attacks on our reproductive rights. May our children not be subjected to a court system that demands that we walk the tightrope of sharing custody and visitation rights with abusive ex-partners. May our constant domestic labor (in addition to full-time paid work) be acknowledged and compensated. May being a single mother (or being raised by one) no longer be synonymous with living in poverty. May we support each other and persevere through the exhaustion and isolation that often accompanies the act of raising children alone. We have a long way to go to change the difficult climate for mothers in this country. We can start with our voices.

Mama Indigo

Elmira Rodriguez

"The best thing you could do is master the chaos in you. You are not thrown into the fire, you are the fire." -Mama Indigo

There is this magic that I can't seem to work. A barrier that i can't seem to penetrate. I've tried

cooing and wooing, ranting and raving, talking and sharing. I've tried dropping it in a love note,

dropping it in a love bomb, whispering sweet nothings and all out raging, but no matter. All for

nothing. Energy spent. Exhausted. Wasted. You won't receive my magic. You won't see my worth.

I have fantasies of slicing open your chest and cracking apart the cages of your ribs with my bare

hands. Visions of extracting your heart from its cavity, severing it from the life force that keeps it

beating, and taking it on a tour. Show it what it has been like to walk the world as me, with love in my

heart for you.

i want to hold your heart in my hands, exploit it of its precious and limited resources while speaking

poison to it, stab it with a smelting sword, drop it in boiling salt water, pulverize it with a jack hammer,

light the mutherfucker on fire, sit back and watch it burn until it's charred through and through. Then,

I would drop it back into its cavity, clasp the cages of your ribs back together, suture your skin, and

let you loose to walk the world like that. Then, I want to tell you that there is really nothing wrong,

that all is well, that you're just freaking out. That it's all in your head.

I want to tell you that the pain that your heart feels is a choice, that you can choose to not feel it, if

you really wanted to. I want to tell you that the condition of your heart is no cause to ask for

accommodation. I want to speak these things to you over and over again, until you begin to whisper

these things to yourself, and I no longer even have to speak a word. Until you make a neurosis out

of hiding the condition of your heart so that I might be spared the gruesome and inconvenient task of

having to witness your pain. I want to hold my friendship on a stick and make you jump for it,

threatening to leave you should you ever so much as speak a word to tell me of how much your

heart hurts or how your feelings in response to my neglect have been fused together with the

tangled and mangled memories of your past. I want to blame you and shame you for your heart

condition. Make you believe that the condition of your heart renders you unworthy of being shown

love or affection. Make you feel like your need for love and affection is a burden; make you beg for it

and ration every little drop that I begrudgingly give you because who knows when I might show you

some again.

I want to leave you to weep out your sorrow alone, in the darkness of our room while I lay blissfully

unaware, next to you in our bed. I want to dispose of you after take that great risk, and let my seed germinate deep in your womb. I want to watch you carry that seed to flower, breaking your body to

give that being life. I want to carry that precious gift like it's an entitled privilege. I want to hold the

weight of that gift as if it's lighter than a feather on my skin and never even once whisper my

gratitude for you and all you have given me. Never once consider all the paths you chose not to walk

so that you could walk this one.

For South Dakota

Marianne Evans-Lombe

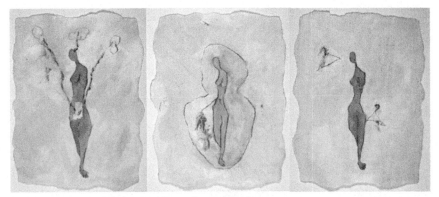

Acrylic and graphite on canvas.

Modern Icon V

Marianne Evans-Lombe

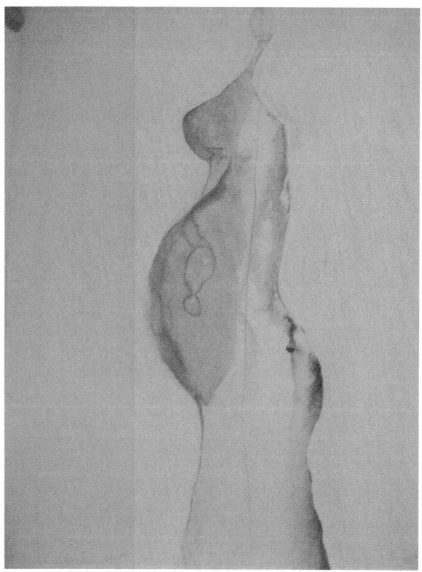

Watercolor, graphite, and collage on canvas.

The Promise of a Ring

Julie Wolfrum

"With this ring, I thee wed,"
Are words I may never say.
But...
I do have a diamond ring.

Thin crosses of gold
Wrap around my finger,
Incrusted with tiny little diamonds
Shimmering like hope in
Newlywed's eyes.

It's from a dollar store.

A gift from a married friend,
"Now it looks like someone really
Does love you."

I wear it on my right hand,
When walking alone.
Finger cloaked in
"Just me," on my thin, unlovable hand.
No one notices.

When I walk with my son,
I switch the ring to my left hand.
Now, I am loved.
Now, my son is loved.

Now, I am family.
With this band, I succeed.
"What a beautiful ring!"
They say
Glancing cordially
At my son.

Why...thank you.

Why is America So Far Behind?

Trista Hendren

THESE LAST YEARS, I have connected with many single moms from around the world. In sharing stories, people were often baffled by how far behind the U.S. Is in comparison to other Western countries. I started to make some of my own comparisons which ultimately led me to begin this project.

As Andrea Dworkin noted ages ago:

> "When one thinks about women's ordinary lives and the lives of children, especially female children, it is very hard not to think that one is looking at atrocity—if one's eyes are open. We have to accept that we are looking at ordinary life; the hurt is not exceptional; rather it is systemic and it is real. Our culture accepts it, defends it, punishes us for resisting it. The hurt, the pushing down, the sexualized cruelty are intended; they are not accidents or mistakes." -Andrea Dworkin

Information on child support is difficult to find, which is baffling considering how many women and children it effects. One of the most comprehensive studies I have found over the years is "Worst Off: Single Parent Families in the United States." This paper compared U.S. single-parent families with single-parent families in 16 other high-income countries.

> "We find that U.S. single-parent families are the worst off. They have the highest poverty rate. They have the highest rate of no health care coverage. They face the stingiest

income support system. They lack the paid-time-off-from-work entitlements that in comparison countries make it easier for single parents to balance caregiving and jobholding. They must wait longer than single parents in comparison countries for early childhood education to begin. They have a low rate of child support receipt.

U.S. single parents have both above average employment rates and above average poverty rates. High rates of low-wage employment combined with inadequate income support explain the paradox of high poverty despite high employment."[17]

Nowhere is the gap more apparent than with maternity leave and sick days. When my son was born, I worked from my hospital bed. A few days after his birth, I rolled him into my office in his stroller and shoved all my files into the bottom to take home. I needed the money. I did not receive any child support at all for the first year of my son's life. I can barely remember that year.

Fortunately, I was able to work from home often and hire my sister as our nanny for his first two years. That said, I still cry when I think about his first year and the enormous loss for both of us.

I remember a wise old crone chastising me for not going after my son's father for child support. I suppose, at the time, I was afraid his father would disappear altogether so I didn't pursue it. She pleaded with me, "What sort of message will this send to your son? When children don't receive child support they associate it

17 Casey, Timothy and Maldonado, Maldonado. "WORST OFF – SINGLE-PARENT FAMILIES IN THE UNITED STATES: *A Cross-National Comparison of Single Parenthood in the U.S. and Sixteen Other High-Income Countries* Legal Momentum: The Woman's Legal Defense and Education Fund. December 2012.

with their own self-worth. A child who receives nothing in child support comes to believe s/he is worth nothing."

When I think about collecting child support—for both myself and women throughout the world—I remember those words. **Our children deserve child support.** Mothers also deserve to be financially supported.

It is extraordinarily difficult to work as a single mother in the United States and make ends meet. There are just not enough social structures in place to ensure that both mothers and children get what they need.

In my case, a high-commissioned job ensured our basic needs were met, but it came at a very high price physically and emotionally. My body broke down, I was sick frequently and I was severely underweight. My son did not get the attention from me his first year deserved.

Try being a working single mom with sick children. In the U.S., It is *impossible*. If you try to maintain a normal job with regular school holidays, sick days and everything else, you will be unlikely to keep it for very long. I remember my ex-father-in-law exclaiming with disgust several times: "I just don't understand why you don't have a *real* job."

(My books don't count, and apparently raising his grandchildren doesn't count either.)

It would be much easier to maintain a "real" job if someone had been co-parenting with me and sharing the weight of sick days and school holidays. But the U.S. is unique as a "high-income" country in not having systems in place that would help single moms.

This became all the more apparent to me when I moved to Norway with my children last year. Here in Norway single moms have special considerations for paid leave. They can legally take more days off work if they have more children or are single mothers. For instance, after working for a qualifying period of four weeks, a person without kids can take five paid days off for sickness.

- If you have one or two children, you can take 10 additional sick days off – and take time off for any doctor/dentist/school appointment with no problem.
- If you have three or more children, you are entitled to 15 days a year.
- If you are a single mom of one or two children, you are entitled to 20 days a year.
- If you are a single mom caring for more than three children, you are entitled to 30 days of paid time off.

There are additional provisions for longer sicknesses. If you have chronically ill or disabled child, you can take ten days in addition for each chronically ill or disabled child. You are also entitled to the same number of days if you work part-time.[18]

---

18 Njarga Berit B. "Så mange sykt barn-dager har du krav på *Dinside*. 2014.

The following chart demonstrates the disparity very clearly.[19]

Table 4. PAID TIME OFF				
	Annual leave (weeks)	Holidays (days)	5 Day Sick Jobholder Absence	5 Day Sick Child Absence
Australia	4	7	5	5
Austria	4.4	13	5	5
Belgium	4	10	5	0
Canada	2	8	0	0
Denmark	4	9	5	1
Finland	5	9	5	0
France	6	1	1	0
Germany	4	10	5	5
Ireland	4	9	0.7	3
Italy	4	13	1	0
Netherlands	4	0	3.5	3.8
Norway	5	2	5	5
Spain	4.4	12	1.2	2
Sweden	5	0	3.2	4
Switzerland	4	0	5	3
U.K.	4	0	0.4	0
U.S.	0	0	0	0
AVG. (excl. U.S.)	4.2	6	3.2	2.3
Median (excl. U.S.)	4	8.5	4.3	2.5

Notice that the averages and mediums listed exclude the U.S., which is the only country of the 16 studied which provides **zero** days of annual paid leave. The study notes:

"Many U.S. employers voluntarily provide paid annual leave, sick days, and holidays but many also do not...Based on the American Time Use Survey (ATUS) of individuals, 32% of single parents and 64% of married parents reported having access to paid leave at their main job in 2011."[20]

19 Casey, Timothy and Maldonado, Maldonado. "WORST OFF – SINGLE-PARENT FAMILIES IN THE UNITED STATES." December 2012.
20 Casey, Timothy and Maldonado, Maldonado. "WORST OFF – SINGLE-PARENT

The study also notes that child care is expensive in the U.S., compared to the other 16 countries where it is generally provided. Single mothers with children under five have a particularly rough time with this, as for "many single parents, actual or potential earnings are too little to pay for child care."[21]

While public education is available for children over five, it generally ends in the early afternoon, leaving a huge gap in the day. In addition, school districts in my home State of Oregon are only in session 165 days a year. [22]

Not to get too far off track, but when you take into account that most people nowadays are forced to drop their kids off at school whether they are sick or well, it also means that children are often sick more frequently. Additionally, when you are already living under the chronic stress of being a single parent, you are also more susceptible to becoming ill. I remember some years where my children and I were sick more often than we were well.

Lastly, of the 16 countries studied, the United States was the only country that did not provide a child allowance, averaging about $150 a month per child. Some countries also provided an additional amount for single mothers.[23]

In Norway, we receive approximately $100 a month per child. This doesn't go very far in today's world—raising children is expensive —but it does help! It is the only time in years that I haven't had to

FAMILIES IN THE UNITED STATES." December 2012.
21 Casey, Timothy and Maldonado, Maldonado. "WORST OFF – SINGLE-PARENT FAMILIES IN THE UNITED STATES." December 2012.
22 Oregonian Editorial Board. "More days for Oregon students, more pay for Oregon teachers: Agenda 2013." *The Oregonian.* August 31, 2013.
23 Casey, Timothy and Maldonado, Maldonado. "WORST OFF – SINGLE-PARENT FAMILIES IN THE UNITED STATES." December 2012.

worry about paying my children's allowance on time and whether or not we can afford to attend birthday parties.

In quite a few of the "high-income" countries, we seem to have lost a sense of community—which would help single moms out more. Many grandparents are working in their later years or live further away. Neighbors and extended family aren't what they used to be. Driven by capitalism, Western societies have become more individualistic—and no one suffers more from this than single moms and their children.

Child support enforcement seems to be one of the biggest obstacles in supporting healthy single-parent families. I highly recommend reading the full study in detail, which is available online. I know in my own life that not receiving child support has been one of the biggest hurdles in raising healthy and happy children.

Looking to Scandinavian countries seems wise in determining the best course of action in reforming child support enforcement in the United States. As *Think Progress* recently noted:

> "As of 2010, all European countries except the Netherlands **guaranteed child support payments** to custodial parents even if the noncustodial parent couldn't pay or could only pay part. Sweden goes even further and has a guaranteed assistance program in which all custodial parents get a child support payment from the government no matter what, and the government then collects what it can from the noncustodial ones. Such a system seems to work — 95 percent of these parents get child support payments."[24]

24 Covert, Bryce. "The Brilliant Idea From Europe That Could Revolutionize Child Support." *Think Progress*. April 16, 2015.

Even though I have remarried—and life is considerably easier in Norway—there is not a day that goes by that I don't have to deny my children something because of lack of child support.

This is not something any of us will likely "get over" for the rest of our lives.

The authors of the "Worst Off" study conclude: "U.S. single-parent families will remain the worst off unless the U.S. expands its family-supporting policies."

Flower Child

Noelle Williams

a flower was offered to me
as I walked the beaten path
that led to nowhere
I hid it deep inside my belly

grow my little one
I whispered now and then
as its petals grew flush
to the walls of my womb

butterflies joined the flower in dance
rejoicing I would speak my heart
singing, humming, smiling
you will bear my name

the truth I could plainly see
I had no garden to place you
no shelter, no home
for I dwelt in a barren wasteland

I traversed a path narrow and hidden
overgrown and hard to go
steadfast in my quest
I plowed on, my aim being true

I knew in my soul
that your birth would herald
the singing of angels
as your love light spread around

you became my hope, my dreams, my salvation
nothing could deter you from my goal
to find a sanctuary
to plant my precious flower

sincere in my promise of protection
I will nurture her till she can stand alone
tall, strong and proud
roots firmly planted in the ground

Lilith

Arna Baartz

Mother Magic

Sierra Melcher

IN THE LAND OF ETERNAL SPRING, Medellin, Colombia, where the sun shines every month of the year and the people are all smiles, Mother Magic has found me.

In the quiet, near dark of early morning, a little voice calls from the foot of the bed, "mas." She wants more. She is hungry. In the half light, I reach for her. "Up" in a soft and delightfully pleading tone that begs compliance. On tip-toes, both arms and one leg already on the bed, pulling the sheets tight and nearly able to climb up herself, she says again, "Up-mama." Her stuffed turtle with her always for comfort. She clings to its tag as I lift her into my enormous empty bed. A smile of triumph glows on her little face. Teeth, so many teeth in that little smile. "Mas," she says and signs bringing her fingers together three times to make sure I understand. She lets her head drop onto my chest. Soft cheeks brush my collar bone. The heavenly ecstasy of a motherly morning embrace. Her heavy body falling into mine without hesitation or resistance. A smile spreads across my whole body, and I sink into the moment. Nothing else could possibly ever matter. This is intoxicating divinity. "Uung, uunhh, unnn." she groans in that distinct "hungry for boob" way, eager with anticipation and desperation. In any other context that sound would unquestioningly sound of sex, but she is hungry, and as I pull up my shirt she squeals and lets out a sigh as she dives in. Both relieved. She draws heavily on the nutrients in my breast and the growing pressure within me subsides. We breathe together in a slow comfortable rhythm. The trust and routine make this morning blend in with hundreds before it; on this morning my

190

mind wanders into the future and recognizes the preciousness of these fleeting moments.

She has only been sleeping in her own bed for a few weeks; *she is growing so fast. How many more times will I get to wake to such a precious greeting? Someday soon, we will be in a rush, off to school and work, or just growing up and wanting different things, wanting more than to snuggle in momma's arms. How could I ever want anything more than this? I couldn't. But I know soon she will transition into yet another phase and be a slightly bigger girl, increment by increment, until she is a grown woman and we will never snuggle.*

And then she bites a little too hard, and I am immediately brought back into the moment. No time to mourn the future or romanticize the present. My startled look meets her startled and slightly mischievous gaze. A half smile in her blue grey eyes. She waits almost as if to see my next move. Time waits. The world shrinks to the space between our faces. Then she breaks the tension. "Get down. Ekk," she says as she rolls and slides down the side of the bed tottering off toward the kitchen. She wants an egg. And so the morning becomes far too real. Hardly 6am and time to cook let alone stand up. I commit. Feet are on the ground. This is happening. No hope of a few more minutes. "Ekk" she beckons. Dressed or half-dressed I slide into my slippers because the tile floor is brutally hard. I scuff towards the kitchen longing for one more minute of horizontal snuggles, but the day wins. Eden wins; she is hungry.

The light of the day greets me and entices me to smile and take a deep breath. There is no hurry and it is gorgeous out already. Is it December or May? Not sure. They are all the same. I love the tropics. Cool fresh sunshine pours in the front window and the birds are arguing harmoniously about something out in the trees.

"Mamma, up. Doodeli." Looks like we are having blueberries for breakfast while the egg cooks.

Thank goodness for the frozen blueberries from the import store. Life in a foreign land certainly has its perks, but for a few things we have to fight. Here frozen blueberries are a cherished treasure. She stuffs one in her mouth and chews. A look of sincere concentration on her face as if tasting this for the first time. Cold. Sweet. Hard, yet chewy. Her eyebrows come together. A look of consternation as if she has made a bad choice. Then delightful. All her teeth showing blue goop as her smile dashes across her face. Another, yes. Covered in blue-purple smears she holds one out to me and I lean in as she feeds me. "Nom, nom, nom." I gobble her hand and the berry too. She squeals with delight and immediately thrusts another berry in my direction. We repeat this game until there are no berries left, just the blueberry war paint on her cheeks, shoulders, pajamas and my left arm. We are ready for our day.

There is no rush. Still no school or *guarderia* to cart her off to. No job to rush off to. We live in the yoga studio I run. While she naps, when she naps, I get something done, or try. But she has hours of exploring before she is ready to crash this morning. So the day lies ahead of us. Full of moments to explore new things, practice new words and totter.

New clothes, socks and shoes. Chubby little thighs hang out of cute ruffles. My girly-girl daughter. I would never have imagined, dripping in pink and polka dots. Striped socks and pink suede dirt scuffed-high tops. The things people buy for babies. I don't look as nearly well put together, but I also believe I will never have sex again, so what does it matter? We emerge into the light of the street and repeat the game to find what we can climb. The steps of the building down the street are a current favorite. The unimaginable joy of climbing up these seven steps to just climb down again. And again, and again. She is my teacher. Teaching me the magic of motherhood. The simplicity of the moment, of every moment. Whether we are climbing, eating, snuggling, bathing or crying. It just is. There is no before and there is no after; there is just the moment. She is my little Buddha master. I am a dedicated student but not... *what is the word*? The mind of a mother is constant and striving. *What is the WORD?* Just on the tip, well not the tip of my tongue. Really, it is in a pile with some other stuff I haven't used in a while in the back right recesses of my mind, like my closet. The point being that I am no great student.

Persistent, attentive, but not yet there. Not getting every lesson or opportunity to be present. Maybe when I am half asleep I am there savoring every moment. But often I drift forward or back. *What will it be like when she is older? What should I say if her father ever shows up? Did I do the right thing? Will we live in Colombia forever?*

"Boom" **WHAT?** I am back in the moment. She tripped and is down. I am needed. I pick her up and brush her off. She is tough and is right at it again. Does she need me or do I need her? Yes. My little teacher pulling me back into the now. The lessons of Mamma Magic are subtle, innumerable and constant. Nothing special and everything miraculous. Everything is both work and play. Learning for us both as we grow up into a family. As we become the people we will be; She becomes this person to be known as Eden, and I am growing into a mother-version of myself. We are a little team. A living, loving mother-daughter team. Teaching each other as we go. Expats in a foreign land like guests or tourists in a home that will never be entirely ours, for better and worse. Visitors. Making each moment even more unique. As a foreigner everything seems odd already, heightening the preciousness of the moment. Hand-in-hand, tottering down the foreign street, our street. A little wobbly and slightly out of place in this familiar home we have made out of nothing; this family we have also made out of nothing. The balance comes from our connection. Sometimes we each fall. Still learning as we go. And when we do we are there to brush each other off and keep on.

Mother magic keeps every moment special, even the monotonous, because we do it together.

A Tiny Screeching Demon

Arna Baartz

she blew in on rotten air
her eyes dark and bitter green
her lips the shade of plum...cresting a wave of lies
a virtual shroud dressing the whore of insecurity
and yes when I peered close I could see a smaller version of myself
mirrored there
a poor child
yet in her case the aging did not produce any smooth rose
but instead vinegar
and like broken branches
losing their way in a flourishing tree
she struggled grey and sharp
growling and gnawing at my children
her magic was ugly and took the long route....
her dirty paws tucked in their wet beds,
and poked at an abscess of miscommunication that grew in one
little boys jaw
she led the way for dead mothers and zombies,
filing proudly past dream catchers....

tiny confused fingers waved, clawing at my throat, pulling at my
feet,
a weak goodbye, off to the house of horrors,
yes it had nice curtains.

~

We watched with eyes as deep as lakes as she drove an axe
through the tender trunk of Joey's tree,
her jealousy shrill that there be a memory there of me.

195

Joey lives in my heart I said and the little ones trusted.
because It is true.

We relied on love, you see, nurtured concepts of forgiveness.
We spoke of people having sadness like a fishing sinker, hanging
from their heart
creating weight that deranges the mind
and causes strange and painful words to swing,
words that have the power to nestle in and fester
and we persevered with love , the only thing we really knew....
in the face of her shaking anxiety and awkward tyre slitting rage
until HE began to notice a pounding, swelling hepatitis,
and finally realised he was using her to kill himself
to distort his own dogeared pain.
To give him credit then,
he didn't linger much longer....
shearing through woody tangle
to extricate himself from the fever of her wailing sex.
Evil stepmothers belong only in fairy tales
they are not real
they do not exist.....not anymore
like tiny screeching demons that lift you by the hair
we faced her
and we killed her with LOVE

How to Notice Red Flags

Molly Pennington

MY FIRST HUSBAND ONCE BROKE HIS NECK by smashing head first into a brick fireplace. "I did it for you," he told me. "That's how much I love you. Instead of hurting you, I hurt myself."

"But you did hurt me," I answered. "The bruises—"

"The bruises aren't from me," he countered. "That's on you. Everything makes you bruise. You can't blame that on me."

Brian (not his real name because he'll find me and sue me) had lots of pronouncements for me: I pushed buttons. I asked for it. I walked into fists. I bruised easily.

I have to tell you that I missed every red flag.

That's just it about the flags. They aren't red. They aren't obvious. They come in like whispers. Like the scent of lilies. They're shaped like chiffon hearts. They are the color of bubbles. They are apologies and proposals. Intensities in the dark. Pleadings. That you must give in to. For love. He tells you it's love. The flags are sinews of shame, stretching slowly, bending to an ache, then finally snapping sometime when you're pretty far away from anything you recognize as home.

In my case, our son was two. He was standing by the stove, watching us. He had always been way too pensive for a baby. Serious. Observant. Clingy.

"You bitch like a fuckin' cow," sneered Brian.

I looked at my son. I met his eyes and his understanding, and finally, my Achilles tore. And just then, when I irreversibly had the fire to leave... it was all just beginning.

When I left, Brian argued. But not about our child. I don't think it had hit him yet. I was the one who took care of the baby after all. Why wouldn't I take him with me? Brian complained about our son anyway. "He doesn't like me. The kid prefers you," he seethed. "He's a baby," I explained. "He doesn't have to give you anything. You give it to him. That's parenting."

When I said this kind of thing Brian looked at me like I was an alien.

I was blindsided when I found out that he wanted our son. Not only that. He wanted him away from me.

I count 14 custody hearings or events over the years. That doesn't include the four-day trial when our son was 12. Or all the psychological evaluations. Meetings with lawyers. Mediators. Court appointees. It also doesn't consider the divorce proceedings. The child support disputes. Usually before hearing officers. Or the final lawsuit—claiming I owed travel expenses from five years prior. I was served those papers a few months after our son turned 18. He was away at college. The lawsuit demanded nearly five figures in cash and also included a motion that I serve time in jail should I be found guilty.

I was not found guilty—so ruled the court, eventually.

Brian instigated each court battle, each hearing, trial and lawsuit
—every single one. And I won them all. When I didn't willingly
concede. I gave in as much as I could. I cut child support to just
$200 per month. I gave him visitation on every weekend and
holiday. I gave in as much as I could. To avoid expense and hassle.
And the expense was considerable.

If you knew the amount you would probably vomit.

The amount is what it would cost to send two students to college.
It's three times the amount of my highest-ever salary. And that
was only to fight some of the battles. I didn't fight on child
support.

Did you know that it costs thousands of dollars in lawyer fees to
compel a person to release their tax returns?

Tax returns he's probably lying on anyway because he was always
like that about money.

I gave all that I could. But I could not give him primary custody of
our son.

"You'll never see him again," said my lawyer. And I knew she was
right.

Brian didn't care about the outcome of court. He was excited by
the idea that I hated it. One time he called me in advance of a
hearing with a custody mediator.

"I want to work this out," he said.

"Me too," I gushed. "Totally. I hate this conflict. It's bad for our son. I want to compromise."

Then I got there. And it started. I had fallen. Again. I'm such a sucker when people act human. I believe in the best in them. I believed that even after years of lies, it was possible for him to become decent.

Forgive me for being such a fool because I've finally forgiven myself.

Only a few years previously Brian had told another mediator that I had been evicted from my apartment for prostitution. His lawyer said it so sheepishly. So apologetically.

"Her neighbors had to petition the landlord to have her removed." Then he leaned forward and lowered his voice, but we could all still plainly hear: "Men coming and going at all hours." I had neglected to bring a lawyer. I was alone. Sitting there for that.

I wasn't a prostitute in case you were wondering.

And no men ever came and went. I was the only graduate student with a child in a competitive doctoral program. I didn't have time for a social life, let alone a side job. I did move out of that apartment. At my own behest. It was a terrible place. I had to find it, secure it and move into it in about 24 hours. It was all I could find. Brian had confiscated my car during the night. A friend flew in to help.

It took at least a year to get on my feet. I moved again to a little house with an upstairs and A/C – on my teaching stipend. But Brian branded me a loser to anyone who would listen.

I look credible. I'm mild. Well-spoken. Conservatively dressed. But so embarrassed. I mean, who marries the kind of person who would say these things?

That's a major theme in our culture. The belief that if it is said, then it must be true. Brian threatened a custody trial for years and then finally followed through. Though I had been on my best behavior to avoid it. To placate him. During my deposition, Brian's lawyer asked me why I "strip nude, get down on all fours, and howl at the moon."

I do not, in case you're curious.

But he said it out loud.

Even after the prostitution allegation, I really did believe that we could compromise. I arrived to the mediation excited, ready for conciliation. As if we could finally move past it. I wouldn't have to say what was on my mind: "That was horrible. I forgive you. Let's move on." My petition would be present, but unstated. Grace.

That was my mood when Brian began the detonation. Even our mediator seemed stunned. Brian has this way of speaking. His eyes narrow. His voice lengthens as if lies cause drawl. There is an undertow of wrath.

He alleged that I was abusing our son. He said that I was abusing our son in the same way that I had always abused *him*. Physical attacks. Emotional manipulation.

I couldn't help it. I cried. And I begged him to please stop lying. To please stop. Just please stop lying.

I didn't know then, but I know now, that a narcissist sees compromise as weakness. It points them not to truce, but to confrontation. And weakness isn't accepted as peacekeeping, but assaultive.

"Please," I sobbed. "Please," I said it again through choking tears. "Stop. Just stop. Don't do this." I almost fell to my knees. And might have if not for the formal setting.

The mediator shifted, embarrassed. This was beyond his scope. The dynamic. The accusations. The strike and then entreaty. Nuclear dysfunction.

"I can't stop," Brian told me. And he smiled.

"You're dangerous." Then he turned to the dumbfounded mediator: "She's a dangerous woman."

I have retained primary custody since the day that I left.

Twice, Brian failed to return our son after visitations, for more than a week each time. That's how long it took to rally my lawyer and a court of law to even begin to act. By then my son was returned to me.

Once our son burst into tears after Brian (with his parents) dropped him off and left. "I thought you didn't want me anymore!" my sweet boy cried. They had refused to allow phone calls. All contact was denied. Not by the courts. By Brian.

Whatever Brian threw—and it was truckloads of never-ending mud—none of it ever stuck. But everybody still had to gather and listen. Allegations are eventually proven baseless, but still, the words have been typed into documents, shuffled through bureaucracy.

I do not have any advice on how to get through it. If you've got millions for lawyers, then you are all set. Unleash them. While you're at it, get a solid therapist for yourself and your child. If your insurance sucks and if you've sold, mortgaged, liquidated and borrowed everything you can, then still, get the best attorney you can. The only thing left to do is endure it with whatever grace you have. It will feel like you don't have any, but you do.

Trust love. Even still after all this, trust love. Figure out your past. Get a degree in red flags that are actually, as discussed, the color and consistency of sugar water. Figure out their every nuance. Think about your own life as a child.

In my younger days, there was a strange, almost dream-like period before these men (Brian was not the first) turned mean and mighty. I try to turn my memory back to the moments before that Big Bang, when I know, when I see... that they are going to hurt me.

It's always been the last thing I'm expecting.

Even the final lawsuit. I thought I was so used to it. So ready. Then my lawyer told me about the motion to send me to jail. It was ridiculous, of course. She would get it dismissed, of course.

You should know that he got me there. It stung.

I didn't realize that he still had it in for me. I'm sure it's just projection or some upside-down fucked-upped-ness like when he told me he broke his own neck to save mine. He knows he belongs in jail, or is in a psychiatric one, so he slaps that onto me. But I was caught off guard. There's a twinge of surprise, a catch in my breath, just like when I was younger, every time, before the storming.

Lucid

Liz Darling

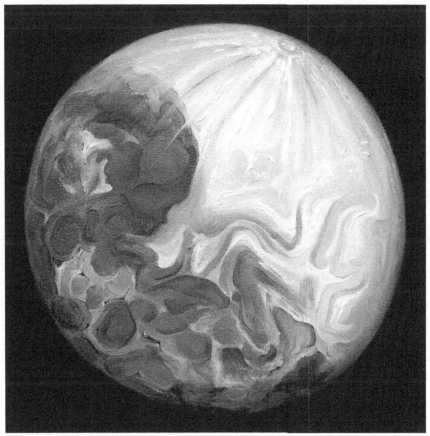

Oil on canvas.

Single Mother, Single Daughter

Karen McLaughlin

just us two
she and me
no awkward third in our skippy-hop dance

parenting requires partnership
one child
one adult

we seesaw
fulcrumed by our mutual dependance
she, my sun; I, her earth

our jokes bewilder them
our made-to-measure language lands as gibberish
our clear collusion confuses

holding the wild and safe space for each other
we are
  unaccountable (except to ourselves)
    free-range (queens of the snuggle zone)
      creators (making the world we need)

unwitting rebels

daring to be

without a he

Single, Woman, Co-parent: Not Abandoned, Not a Slut, Just a Human Being

Leslie

A FEW DAYS AGO, I found myself speaking with a colleague whom I have known for nearly 20 years. She inquired into my experiences as a mother, the well-being of my child, and how our life was unfolding. The California sun shone down on us as I described my adventures of raising a toddler--a constant process of adjusting and attuning as my child grows more into herself, and as all the people around her come to know her and her needs. Since she was six weeks old, I've had the experience of my daughter being away from me for hours, even days, at a time. When people hear this, they tend to ask how old she is. No matter her age, their response is usually "Wow, I couldn't do that," or, with more judgment, "How can you do that?" The assumption is usually made that a mother should be the primary parent with her child all of the time. My response? "She's with her father," just where she needs to be.

I am constantly grappling with the stereotypes associated with gender roles and parenting, and with the expectations around parenting "norms." I never intended to be a biological mother, but when I discovered I was pregnant, I listened as attentively as I could to my inner voice, to the voices of support around me that advocated for the right choice for myself and any future child that I brought into the world. I listened when the man who helped me create this child told me quite simply, "We'll make it work." There were no promises of how, but the assurance was made that, together, we'd find a way.

Like many women before me, I was unintentionally impregnated[25] by a friend. A momentary act of playful pleasure became a commitment of extraordinary terms and proportions. It's happened to millions before me, and will continue to happen to millions after I am gone. Despite the circumstances of her conception, I can comfortably say this: my child came into the world deeply loved by both her parents, both of whom were single, and who were not romantically involved with one another or anyone else at the time of conception or birth.

Nevertheless, these circumstances are not a pass for lack of responsibility and accountability.

Throughout my pregnancy and these first two years of parenting, I have found myself encountering countless stereotypes, assumptions, and divisive, unconscious behaviors and comments that beg conversation.

On Unintentional Pregnancies

When I began to share that I was pregnant, I become subjected to a series of responses from my friends and community members— many who self-identify as open-minded, progressive, and welcoming. I quickly discovered that as the female counterpart in the creation of new life, I was treated differently: some stopped talking to me, or taking my ideas in our work or conversations as seriously; others became snarky or rude. Because of the number of mutual friends, our common work place, and overlapping projects, I witnessed how, in contrast, my child's father was treated. I had many conversations in which it became clear that, somehow, people had always left room for the possibility that a woman might become accidentally[25] pregnant by him, and so his

25 There are a myriad of pregnancy and parenting-related terms that disturb me. This one is such a term.

"slip-up" was accepted. He was granted instant forgiveness and acceptance. I, on the other hand, had somehow sinned greatly. I was the irresponsible one, the pariah, the one who made a "stupid" choice.

My baby's father? Forgiven, teased. Few understood why this double-standard bothered me so much. They failed to grasp that this difference in response wasn't based on who we were and our personalities, but, rather, was a perpetuation that women who have sex and get pregnant unintentionally don't know their bodies, make poor choices, should "know better." Men do not need to know their bodies. They sow their wild oats and are free —to come and go, to make a choice. We live in such a strange world: the support granted my child's father for his transgressions was never given me, because of how our sexuality was viewed, and because of how our actions were contextualized.

I've called people out as kindly as I can on the double-standard, expressed sorrow for being reduced from the intelligent, striving, and caring person I aim to be, to a simple slut-who-made-a-mistake narrative. I'm not that: I'm a woman who made a choice in an instance, who took responsibility for it with the resources she had, and who has tried to continue to cultivate as much honesty and integrity as she could around her unintended pregnancy. For other reasons, my journey has been a painful one at times, with plenty of health challenges, ample opportunity for defeat, and an existential personality that compels me to question my choices. But it's also been a joyful and growth-inspiring one. I have faced, accepted, and then embraced the path I am on, and the relationships I have chosen. *Because I chose them all.*

Co-parenting: Seeking a Clearer Definition

When my child's father sought to understand my parenting needs and expectations, he stood by my side first as my friend and second as the (potential) father of my child. I was clear that as much as I loved my friend, I couldn't marry him when he asked. This form of relationship was not our path. I did, however, want to find a way to be committed to our relationship as parents together, to embark as friends who had created life, and to find a way to co-carry the responsibilities of raising and guiding that life as best as we could, playing to our strong suits. This meant not equal responsibility in a 50-50 custody agreement, but in a relationship that took both of us, our realities, our goals and the demands upon us and our energies, as well as the needs of our child, into account. This is a lofty goal. I am constantly trying to determine what it means to co-parent. I don't have a tangible, simple answer. It's a constantly evolving process with great highs and lows.

Contrary to the common associations with the term "co-parenting," we are not divorced, nor separated, nor do we equally share the responsibilities of caring for our child. We strive for equity, and most importantly, for ensuring that our child is seen, guided, included, and loved by her community. She's integrated into both of our busy realities—she sometimes comes to work with us, travels with us, she cooks and cleans with us, walks with us, plays with us, learns with us.

I am attracted to the word "co-parent," because it implies a collaborative parenting model. I still cannot give a concrete answer to my child's father what I mean by "co-parent," but we're raising our child together. I want to do away with the stories: my daughter doesn't live in a broken home—we never had a home together. Ours is not an *alternative* relationship form. Many friends have had sex and conceived and found their way to raise their children in loving and supportive ways. We knew that we would have many challenges: our patterns would either undermine or serve us; our needs would conflict at times; the demands on our time would make scheduling and planning and communicating challenging. But we've stuck to a simple tenet: We'll make it work.

A Guiding Light

While I was pregnant, I recall reading an article on co-parenting[26] that helped me get clearer about my ideals for this newly-forming relationship. I didn't want to just do drop-offs and pick-ups and schedules, I didn't want to have to make all the decisions on my own, and I didn't want either of us to be alone in the experience of raising a child; I wanted to spend time together, to make memories, to be able to call for help. So, with some edits, I began to work with these principles:

> 1) Set the intention to have a compassionate and supportive co-parenting relationship.
> 2) Remember the qualities that you admired about your ~~ex~~ friend as a parent~~, when you were both still feeling the bliss~~ in easier times.
> 3) Talk to your kids about your ~~ex's~~ friend's great qualities.
> 4) Try not to talk to all and sundry about a decision that you two, as parents, need to make.
> 5) Don't dump your new partner's needs and feelings on your ~~ex~~ friend.
> 6) Think about how you can make your ~~ex's~~ friend's life easier whilst still having your own needs and wants met.
> 7) Appreciate the parenting skills you see working in your

26 Emma Bathie, *9 Ways to Co-Parent Like a Grown-up*, HuffPost Divorce, 3/28/2014.

~~partner's~~ friend's new relationship, if there is one.

8) Keep to previously agreed schedules and arrangements yet be open-minded and flexible enough to realize that plans will occasionally have to be changed.

9) Do the inner work that needs to be done to help you be the best co-parent you can be and prepare you for the next relationship you might want to have.

So, now I had a working rubric, but I was still frustrated by the dialogue around co-parenting as friends. Whenever people find out that I am close friends with my co-parent, the follow-up is surprise and then, "Why aren't you together?" Why, indeed. Why aren't you with every person you've ever cared about? I understand this question, and I also yearn for the social narrative to change. I yearn to not have to witness the ripple of confusion when I quietly inform someone that, "No, we never were together." "And yet you are friends?" "Yes, yes, we are. We care deeply about one another." Why, oh why is this such a *thing*?

When I express my consternation to my co-parent, he replies pragmatically: "Tell them something that they can understand, then, if you don't want to explain our reality. Just tell them we're no longer together." But, I begin to protest, that's not *true*, and I shouldn't have to tell a lie for my truth to be acceptable.

And here is why I think that this is such a problem, such a "thing." I am a single woman who is raising a child. I post photos and stories on my social media profiles, sharing my life with my community. When I am tired, when it's the middle of the night and I lie in bed listening to my child's contented sighs, I tend to get philosophical. I share my struggles and questions—as a woman, and as a human being; I did this before I carried life and I will probably do so until I die. For those who are not close to me, their comments often encourage me to be strong, to keep on fighting, to believe in myself. Why? Because I post a photo of my child here or there, I rarely tag or refer to her father (it's just not something we do), and so, the picture for many is that I am on my own. So let me say this: far from it. I may be lonely, and in that moment I may be alone with my child, but I am not raising my child alone.

And here the gender stereotypes emerge, again, biting at my heels: as an unmarried, unattached woman, I must have been abandoned to deal with my pregnancy and child. I must have to fight for my child's father to be in her life and to "pull his weight." The truth is so far from this, and when I try to explain—any time I try to explain—I find that I become another gender stereotype: the defensive, overused, overworked woman.

So, please, hear me out once more. I know I've said it all, but, I need to say it again.

Woman, Mother

I am a single woman. I am a mother. I live on my own. I work to provide for us both. I am existential in nature, and idealistic in my hopes for the future. I have long felt that the term "single parent" is inadequate.

And, while I currently have no romantic partner, I have a partner in my co-parent. I am deeply appreciative of and committed to this man who has not just stood by my side and given me a chance, but who has afforded me every opportunity to live my life and to not let the unintentional creation of my daughter's life serve as an excuse for not living my life my way. He reminds me time and again that I am free—free to come, free to go, just as the world reminds him that he is, over, and over, and over again. My co-parent has only ever asked one thing of me: to be safe and to let him know where I am. "Go be yourself. Do what you must to be you, don't let me or our reality stand in your way."

In this, I am lucky. When I compared myself to the mothers I met in my Post Partum Depression support group, I always left thinking, "Thank you, thank you, *thank you*." My co-parent has so clearly helped us from not stepping into roles that weren't ours to perform. I never had someone at home who expected me to have a clean house with dinner on the table and a happy baby who wasn't screaming, to always be happy, or to work. I had someone who just needed me to be me.

Unphased by the possible challenges that may be presented by a nursing infant, he took, and continues to take, his daughter with him readily, for hours and days on end. This, I learn time and again, is unusual. Few fathers I know care comfortably for their children at such a young age for more than a few hours. My co-parent's "We will make it work" attitude has allowed me to work far from my home, and to know that my child is safely cared for.

I didn't realize how unique this arrangement was until one day my co-parent came to pick up our seven-month-old daughter from my work, and a colleague (a grown man of 45 with three children) commented, "I could never do that." When I asked what he was referring to, he said, "Take one of my children when they were that young. It's just not something I could do." I remember feeling dumbfounded by the idea that this was an issue for a parent of three—and the imbalance in roles that that must place in his parenting relationship. I was overwhelmed by a rush of gratitude at realizing that when I say I have a co-parent, whatever challenges and inconsistencies and assumptions and unfinished conversations we have, I have someone who will take on an equal measure of the work when I cannot, who will provide as much as he is able without complaint.

When I look at those women I know who *are* single moms, I admire them for their strength and their courage. I cherish their tenacity and appreciate them for the tears that they shed, the joy the exude, their capacity to be there so readily all of the time. I am *not* a single mom. I am also not an angry or abandoned divorcee or ex-girlfriend. I know those, too. Their stories have their places, and theirs are equally incredible. But they have something I don't: a socially-relatable category, despite its commonality. My reality, my words, have no identifiable narrative, no associated cultural picture that I can offer without explanations. And, maybe it shouldn't. Maybe we don't need boxes and narratives and categories anymore. But do we have the language to describe what my reality *is* then in a way that people can get without lengthy explanations?

I am a woman, I am a nurturer and a community builder and a dreamer. I cry and laugh and get angry. I climb trees and fix broken things. I am a single woman. I am a mother. I am a teacher. I am a co-parent.

When I find myself up against the "mother who cares more about work than her child" story, or scrolling past yet another, "You're doing a great job, you're so courageous to be doing this on your own," comment, I find myself asking: How can I step into *this*, how can *we* step into this, and not be judged or slammed up against a myriad of assumptions about our parenting based on a presumed notion of what my role as a mother *should* look like?

My daughter has two engaged, committed parents; she has two homes; she is loved by many. My hope is that she in the future will not have to explain her reality because it's a "thing," but that she will be able to freely come and go between her homes, to call upon her parents in times of need and celebration. I hope she will experience what happens when two people stand together, as best as they can in each moment, in order to "make it work," and that that serves as an example of tenacity, love, and commitment that gives her hope when she needs it, and strength when she wants it.

Our relationship is not always easy. We have disagreements, we get tired, we have needs that go unmet. But I can say this: we forgive, we try again. So far, raising a child is not the hardest thing I have done; rather, finding my way all the time through everyone's feelings and thoughts, their expectations and assertions about how I should be as a mother and how my child's father should be as a father, is the hardest thing I've had to do.

What I am doing isn't brave, it just is what it is. I want to raise my child to be brave and creative and kind, and to do that, she needs both her mother and her father because she chose both of us. I want to pave a path for my daughter so that she can create relationships that are reflective of who she is as a person and not just who society projects her to be. I want her to see her parents as individuals who take responsibility for their choices and who are supported by loving, kind, and open-minded people. To do this, I need to question and invite conversations around these experiences, to continue to support her father to give her baths and read her stories and take her for long walks and share his pizza with her and to know that when she's tired, they curl up together to sleep, just as I do. And that we both do this in our own way.

My intentions are simple: be the best parent I can be, learning what I'm capable of, discovering where my limitations of knowledge and experience are, not because of what society tells me they are, but because of who I am and how much more growing I need to do. This is what it is to be human: not just woman, not just mother, and definitely not alone.

A One-Handed Poem Written While Breastfeeding

Nile Pierce

My Jasmine plant casts a shadow of a phoenix bird,
Or a Benu, if you're into hieroglyphics
The Roman eagle, cast as the gold standard by which I march
Rhythmically, to the beat of mine own super bass drum
The singer of serpent's songs
A breather of angel's breath
I mime social niceties just to get by without interrogation
The swan, neck outstretched, wings open
Wide, with tempered strength, perched high atop the shadow tree
The scent of my Jasmine plant reminds me of
How sensual I am
Despite the androgynous haircut
I cut my hair to get rid of every last bit of negativity,
I let it go in the Ganges,
I gave it to God
But then She gave it back to me
And told me to make paintbrushes
So in my spare time I do art
And sew quilts made of transmutations
Some might call it 'shabby chic' but I call it *necessary*
I Am a single mother
Through birth, I died to the world of men
I have been made new
In the sight of the Most High
Empress guided by eagles
Most Holy Mother, Lady of One Thousand Names
Of Mountain, and Thunder, and Wherewithal
And Flame
You are the featherbed I lay my head in to rest

You are the fire that consumes me as I rise
And I rise
From these flames, with these flames
I drink the crystal clear Truth from Your stream of Mercy
You give me Hope, Life
I lie awake at night wondering how I can better serve you,
How I can be a better mother
I've seen your signs in the clouds
I've watched as you were there for me
As you spoke to me sweetly in silence
You've heard my cries
You know my pain, my brokenness
You are the only one who knows me
You knew me in the sandbox when I was a child,
When I spoke with my heart but didn't know who you were,
I knew you were listening, I knew you were pure
Like me
We rise together
We seal spiritual victories
And sit, meditatively
Singing songs in ancient tongues
To rhythms that resemble the best rap records
Without the capitalism and misogynistic bullshit
Breathing in the Jasmine air like
[inhale] and [exhale]
We Three are One and We rise
Grabbing laurel leaves on the way up
We go
In Love
Up, up, up
We go
In Love.

Angry Medusa

Nile Pierce

Those of us,
the single mothers,
The war veterans, battle worn,
the recipients of brainwash techniques
that've severed the heads of millions of Medusas
Since the dawn of time, or, more appropriately
Since the beginning of male-dominated everything

FUCK THEM and the Near Eastern horses they rode in on
With their hipster beards, birds in hand
Like the Goddess would accept an offering
From someone who rapes and kills her Daughters!
FUCK THEM and their 30-male party
FUCK THEM and their entitlement to our bodies
FUCK THEM and their hatred for Purity
And Life-Giving Power
FUCK THEM for thinking we are property

BITCH, YOU DON'T OWN ME
I AM MY OWN
I, AND A THOUSAND OTHER WOMEN WILL TAKE YOU DOWN
WITH FIERCE PHOENIX FIRES
AND SPIRITUAL MIDWIFERY AND HERBALISM
WE WILL INVOKE HECATE AND
SEND THE UNDERWORLD AFTER YOUR ASSES LOL

Hell yeah I'm motherfuckin angry
We got a *right* to be angry after thousands
Of years of your BULLSHIT.

The Cycle

Katherine Belliel

THE ANGER WAS PALPABLE. My heart felt like it was beating out of my chest. As the rage roiled over me in waves, I stood my ground. Feeling both betrayal and relief. My grandpa had never talked to me like this in life. Had never raised his voice nor hand to me. But, I always knew he had towards others. My dad and my grandma for sure. But never to me.

"What do you think you are doing?"

"Who do you think you are?" he snarled at me, the words smacking my face like a blow.

"You think you are special?" he continued, while I started shaking. Doing nothing to stop the tirade. Tears rolled down my cheeks. This was the man who had taught me all I knew about birds, bought me my first premium set of binoculars so I could birdwatch with him up at the lake north of our house in Michigan. The man who never missed a dance recital, band concert, or colorguard performance. He would take me to cherry orchards before my birthday, lifting me up so I could reach the best cherries on the highest branches. Yet here he was now, spitting venom in my face. Deep down I knew that I could wake up from this.

My eyes snapped open and I sat up in bed, in the new flat I had rented a mere two months before. The long eyelashes on my six year old son barely fluttered as I tried to catch my breath and wiped sweat from my face. The sickly smell of fear-sweat permeated the air. Only my two tabby cats stared at me with concern from the end of the bed, both giving me slow, loving blinks before turning on the motors to deep, reassuring purring.

You're going to be OK.

The worst is over.

I told myself over and over. But my nightmare had me wide awake, and I abandoned any pretense of going back to sleep. Like any good cat that senses his mistress is in distress, the younger of my two tabbies, Finn, padded over to me and rolled to my side wanting to play. Why not? I thought to myself, as I played his favorite game of pushing my hand in between his ears while he rolled around trying to paw it off. Fake biting my hands and smacking me with paws with his claws retracted. I suspected Finn of having a sensory processing disorder. Watching and analyzing my cats helped distract me from the troubles of my own life, and made me smile as well. Finn's antics weren't enough to make me forget my dream, though. You see, my beloved grandpa had died suddenly 13 years ago. I remember getting the phone call from half the world away, while sitting in my office in Istanbul, Turkey.

Grandpa was dead. Heart attack, they thought.

I never got to say good-bye. If I had known he would die, I would have postponed my move from Michigan to Turkey. In the years after his death, stories about him would trickle out here and there from various family members about grandpa's temper. Rages he used to get into. And everyone would laugh, including me, although I had never born the brunt of it. So why this dream? Why now?

I looked around at my bedroom, grateful to have my bed-frame and mattress. I had spent the past year secretly working hard, saving whatever I could, in order to leave my husband of seven years. Seven years of emotional and at times physical abuse. One week of hiding out, sleeping on rolled up mattresses on the floor, while my lawyer set things in motion to keep me safe and file for divorce. My Turkish husband had been shocked, claiming this had come out of nowhere, despite repeated threats that I would leave him over the years. My voice didn't matter, it never had, really. While my husband was at work one day I quickly hired a moving company, snuck back into the house, and moved half of the stuff to my newly rented flat. Alone. In a foreign country, and in my second language, with a child in tow.

From the moment I decided to marry my Turkish husband and remain in Turkey, a country I had known and loved for several years, I had already researched what I would need to do in case of divorce. Like many women who marry into and move to a predominantly Muslim country, the dire warnings from concerned American friends and family seem like they came from the notorious book, *Not Without My Daughter*. I was nothing like the author, Betty Mahmoody. And Turkey wasn't Iran, I would say to comfort others. Yet looking back, I see the signs that my relationship must have already been unsafe, if I was already planning a way out. The abuse had always been there, that's for sure. I was just hoping it would stop after a time. A surprise pregnancy after the honeymoon (how cliche) should have only made things better. But instead, it made things worse. Before the birth of my son, my sense of normal was definitely skewed in terms of physical and emotional abuse. The massive postpartum depression I experienced was not just a hormonal issue; I now see that only after becoming a mother, did I truly understand a lot of the emotional and physical trauma I had experienced as a child. My initiation as a mom became fraught with not just typical new mother stuff, but also filled with what I now see were PTSD reactions to what I had endured as a child. And how I didn't want to do the same with my son, but yet I knew no other way. I wanted to know, but my inner spirit was at war, and I was exhausted. Add to that my husband, rather than emotionally support me, chose instead to kick me while I was down. My stress and grief manifested itself in unexplained health problems, autoimmune disorders, and weight gain. The physical and emotional abuse got worse. Except, after I gave birth, I too fought back both emotionally and physically.

Lengthy visits back to the US to visit my family on the surface seemed OK, but there was always an undercurrent of resentment and hostility. The last visit home I gathered the courage to tell my parents I was leaving my husband. It did not go well. From the moment I broke the news, it got awkward.

"What do you think you are doing?"

"Do you seriously think you can do this?"

"Who do you think you are?"

I had practiced for weeks before telling them, and gave my prepared answers as best as possible. Then watched as they stepped back. From responsibility, offers of help, concern, whatever. Making an obvious point about it as well. Only one nasty fight before I left for Turkey. As my dad berated me and I stopped talking, just took his verbal barrage while he sat on the couch, head bopping, accusatory finger raised, I checked out. Felt my soul duplicate, and another Katie step across the room, watching from afar and guiding me.

"This isn't about you," she whispered to me.

"Your situation is making him confront things from his past, and you are bearing the brunt of it," Katie-across-the-room continued. I felt a strange sense of calm. I stemmed my tears and let the tirade just wash over me until it was finally over. And my dad apologized, kissed me, and said good night. And we just all pretended that it never happened, that his horrible words were never spoken.

But they were. And it wasn't OK. It made me realize the shackles that I had been chained to while living in the US. In this environment, I had subtly been groomed to expect, even crave, this kind of abuse from a partner. I found it, although my soul had always rebelled against it even as a child. My years of health issues can surely attest to that, and I believe the two are deeply related. Strangely enough, I have always felt stronger in Turkey, a deeply patriarchal society. So much so that I am not sure I would be able to go through with my divorce should we have lived in the US.

Living as an expat in Turkey, it is taken for granted that my family's lack of involvement is due to distance. It gives both them and me an easy way out. Since Turkish is my second language, I speak in a much more direct manner than I speak English. That means I am able to express myself more honestly, because I don't know the subtle niceties to soften the blows into a palatable white lie. So I saved my money. Rented a flat, moved out, and filed for divorce. A whirlwind six months that while stressful, also became the first time I felt myself able to breathe. To live. To taste. The first few nights in my new home, while sleeping on the floor, I slept so deeply and soundly it scared me. Surely I should be restless, given this uncertain time of my life? I rushed to a nearby hardware store and purchased a carbon monoxide detector, certain that here had to be a reason for my deep sleep. Yet there was nothing externally wrong. Until tonight, and the awful nightmare of my beloved grandpa.

I was saying no, and somewhere grandpa's spirit was not okay with that. It was a warning to me, that as I delved into my own abusive past, I had to also respect the abuse my father most likely witnessed and endured. And that, while I can not personally heal either of them, in a way healing myself and stopping the cycle of abuse with my son can bring a necessary peace to us all. Finn must agree as he purrs at my side, heavy deep purrs that pull me back toward sleep better than the Valerian supplements I used to take for years.

I love my husband, my dad, my grandpa. I can see the damaged children that they were, and I send hugs to those confused children. Yet that doesn't mean I have to accept their abuse toward me anymore. I have stepped back from all of them, trying to take the time to love myself instead, something that had previously seemed so selfish and narcissistic. It's not just taking my son out of an abusive home that can change the cycle. I have to also show him how it's okay for a woman to love and care for herself. As I drifted back to sleep I talked to grandpa's spirit. Told him how much I loved him, how much I missed him. That I hoped to see him in my dreams again soon. But, I was aware of his abuse toward others, and it was not OK. He was forgiven, but he needed to understand that I was living the consequences of his behavior. Abuse doesn't always just directly affect those abused, it trickles down and generations feel the fallout. I still love and cherish his memory, and always will. But this dream was a wake up call that my path to healing dealt—not just with the abuse I experienced from my husband—but my father, and indirectly from my grandfather as well.

Melting Glaciers

Ihla Nation

*"Discrimination toward women has gone underground,
invisibly weaving itself into the fabric of judicial, political, and
social institutions. The Powers That Be have become wary, subtly
discriminating in imperceptible ways.
It's insidious and scary. . ."*
-Ihla Nation "Then, Now, When"
Woman's Way: The Path of Empowerment[27]

I am 65. After my son, Mike, graduated from high school, I didn't
think of myself as a single parent. After 16 years of single-
parenting, I was no longer responsible for his daily life. He was
grown-up and independent. As time flowed, I realized I am *still* a
single parent. His need for my advice and guidance comes less
frequently, but hasn't disappeared. Parenting never ends. It just
takes on a softer hue.

Mike was two when I divorced my husband. It was 1972 and I was
21. During our less than 3-year marriage, my ex-husband, Bill, had
been through 12 jobs and spent 9 months unemployed. I thought I
could do better on my own. I was intelligent, ambitious,
hardworking, and held big goals. What could stand in my way if
my energy wasn't spent dealing with an immature relationship?

Patriarchy could. This phenomenon had yet to be named in my
mind, but I felt its oppression like a constant asthma attack. My
attempts to better our lives felt like wading through a swampy

---

27 Nation, Ihla. "Then, Now, When" Woman's Way: The Path of Empowerment
(Lynn Marlow, Publisher) Summer, 1995, Boulder, Colorado.

bayou requiring vigilance to avoid the deadly snakes. Sometimes it was an overwhelming deluge that spit out mud and dirty water on every aspect of my life.

It was a power I had yet to acknowledge, kept me pigeonholed in low-paying jobs, interfered with higher educational opportunities, and frequently laughed in my face when I spoke out against the injustices it caused. Patriarchy has metamorphosed through the decades. But it continues to bleed into every aspect of single mothers' lives, infecting the quality of life for her family.

After my divorce, I seldom received the piddly $100-a-month child support the court had ordered Mike's father to pay. When Bill did pay, it was because I called him and made the trip to wherever he might be living to get the money. I would arrive and he wouldn't answer the door. I would go home and try again later. Or Kathy, his second wife, would answer the door and say he was working and hadn't left the money. Once Mike, who had been there on a rare visit, told me his dad was actually hiding in the bedroom.

The back child support was in arrears almost three years. My attorney's attempts to get this resolved failed so he told me there was nothing more he could do. The county support division, whose responsibility it was to ensure that fathers upheld their obligations, was essentially useless. I lost my patience. I filed papers with the court and, because Bill didn't bother to show up to the hearing, he was ordered to spend 15 days in jail and pay up. My guilt over sending my son's father to jail dissipated when I learned later he was out on work release every day. I was told he'd paid what was required to get out of jail, but the $3300 didn't arrive in the mail. After weeks of tracking it, I learned Bill only had to pay court costs. The judicial system took care of itself, but not my son. The back support was never received.

227

After this, Bill *mostly* managed to pay child support—if I called and made the trip to get it. I considered myself lucky. Three of my closest friends were single mothers also. Two of them never received a dime in child support. One got the occasional small cash from her ex-husband when he tried to bribe her for sex. Luckily she was never sucked into that drama.

In the seventies, only 20% of all women got any child support. Often the court let the father off scot free, not issuing any orders for support. Children teetered on the verge of abject poverty, victims of white male America's pervasive power. If the father was ordered to pay child support, many men ignored it. Sadly a popular attitude was that women weren't using the money for the children, but living high on the hog and spending it on themselves. After three years, 50% of fathers who originally met their obligation, no longer paid anything.

I worked two or three jobs to keep us housed and fed. As the woman's movement progressed, I did see improvement. There was an emphasis on assistance for displaced homemakers to return to school for higher education. I took advantage of that opportunity and completed my bachelor's degree in social work. Between academic scholarships and grants, I walked away after graduation owing only $600 in student loans.

But then came the shock. I'd chosen social work not only because it aligned with what I wanted to do, but because I assumed it would be friendlier to women. To my dismay, I learned that 80% of administrators in the social services system were men, mostly white, though there was the rare exception. Women outnumbered men in the field by about 4 to 1. What could possibly explain this imbalance?

A few years later I wanted to move into computer programming which then in its infancy already paid several times what I earned in social work. The University of Denver sought to bring non-traditional students into the burgeoning field through a special intensive program for 15 applicants. During a panel interview, I was asked how I would succeed in this course when I had single-parenting responsibilities. What would I do about child care? I explained I had graduated from college with honors as a single parent. The questioner was reminded by another panelist that this question couldn't legally be asked. But my application received no further consideration. If single mothers weren't non-traditional in this field, who was exactly?

As I worked diligently at each of my jobs, I would butt headlong into attitudes toward women that impacted my ability to provide my son with the quality of life I desired. Attitudes by men and male-dominated systems had yet to implement the laws recently established to help women achieve equal opportunities and pay.

Even in the mid-nineties, patriarchy publicly prevailed. My promotion to Customer Service Manager was given to a young man who was unable to get to work on time, sometimes arriving hours late. He had two company computers stolen out of his car in just a few months. He went on a service call to repair a customer's network where he caused their whole system to crash. They were unable to do business for two days. My boss and owner of this small computer company gave this technician my long-awaited job. He told me he didn't know what to do with him (fire him maybe?). I was too shocked to respond. I left his employment shortly thereafter. Back in low-paying temporary jobs with no benefits, the financial struggles to survive returned.

Over the years I watched as the tentacles of the patriarchal octopus clamped onto women's lives holding them underwater.

But the waters became murky. There was the appearance that women were making progress, and they did to some degree. Inequality became difficult to discern. In rare instances, women earned opportunities and were paid commensurate with male co-workers. Many employers, however, in "smoke-filled back rooms" continued old practices by remodeling the company structure so women were unaware they were being discriminated against. An invisible glass ceiling was now installed.

Today in 2016, the Denver city attorney's office is being sued because a long-time female lawyer in an administrative position discovered she was paid thousands of dollars less than male counterparts. To make it more painful, one of the male attorneys she supervises, is one of those males. My last full-time employer covered his tracks by issuing an ultimatum—anyone caught discussing salaries with any other employee would be immediately terminated. Need anyone ask what the company was hiding?

Not all patriarchy is well-hidden though not for lack of trying. The most personal patriarchal attitudes are painfully shown in the statistics of domestic violence. Or the 400,000 rape kits that sit on shelves in police departments unprocessed. The statistics of rape in the military are horrifying. How dare they bury women alive by ignoring shameful secrets.

One need only look at the U.S. Congress, that greatest gathering of the Old Boys' Network outside Harvard University. There it is in black and white (mostly white). This supposedly august body makes decisions that impact women's daily lives, often not positively. What assistance should they allow and what should women have to do to get it? What will their education cost? Will children on the lower end of the income scale be *given* school lunches?

". . . like racism, patriarchy still exists. And just like racism, it often manifests in casual ways that tend to go unnoticed by the majority of people." (Shannon Ridgway, *Patriarchy and How It Shows Up for Everyone,* 2013).

But in spite of my ranting, I have hope. When I started on my journey as a single parent, women couldn't get credit in their own names, were scarcely seen in law schools, couldn't participate in school sports, didn't dare dream of being astronauts, and were only found in legislatures transcribing the words of men. Now a woman can own her own business, become governor, freely discuss sex and orgasms, get quality health care designed for women, and speak her mind on the floor of the Senate.

Still women have to fight for control of their own bodies, are paid 2/3 of what a man makes, and have to fight for equality in important arenas of our culture. The many years of fighting battles and attempting to overcome the disadvantages of this system has left me in a disadvantaged position. I never caught up with the income of two-parent families and suffer the consequences even now. But thanks to heroic women, dedicated activists, and a few good men, the patriarchal glacier is slowly melting. Progress is being made. Though I caution let's not erase patriarchy by becoming ***them***.

Everything I needed to know about the 2016 Presidential Election I learned in Family Court

Rhonda Lee Case

With his ten year old son at his side, Trump made his triumphant victory speech on November 9th. His son, Barron (whom Melania refers to as "little Donald"[28]) stood blinking and bleary-eyed. Mother was not in the picture. Birgitta Sunderland tweeted: "Why on earth is Barron Trump up at 3 am? That kid is falling asleep on stage. He's ten. So good parenting is not his policy."

The following essay is dedicated to my late son, Louis. He was just ten years old when he bravely began to disclose that he had suffered years of abuse by his father.
~ May his memory be a blessing.

When this meme popped up on Facebook, I laughed and cringed simultaneously. As a veteran of the Custody Wars, having served

---

28 According to an interview she gave for parenting.com.

seven terms of duty on the frontline, having lost a child to death on the battlefield, and suffering from chronic, complex PTSD as a result, this struck a raw nerve. The young people of America — the vast majority of those age 18 to 35 — were absolutely right. They knew. It was Grandpa Bernie who had our best interests at heart. Sadly, children's voices are rarely if ever heard in custody disputes, almost never in those where domestic violence is a factor. A protracted, acrimonious, contentious and wildly bizarre political spectacle has played out in America. These adjectives are also used to describe high conflict custody cases. Millions of Americans are experiencing feelings of disbelief, dread, numbness, or anxiety, perhaps even physical symptoms, the real result of months of accumulated psychic and emotional stress. Too many single mothers know this pain and shock and sense of helpless-ness all too well. We may be experiencing it again as "déjà-vu" or what feels like a flashback as we consider our absurd new political reality. The man who actually lost the popular election is now dubbed in Doublespeak, our "President *Elect*." Thousands of protective parents in the United States, myself among them, have awakened on other days wondering if our new reality wasn't perhaps all a bad dream. Surprised at how much courage was required just to face this strange new day, we awakened feeling scared sick but determined not to give in to despair, for our children's sake.

A mother somewhere in America today is seated in a courtroom where she will learn that it is now court order and law that she send her child the next day into the "care" of a known abuser. Should she refuse, she will face criminal charges and/or loss of the right to parent her children at all. Americans today can think about taking their children to a country where sanity still prevails. Thousands were indeed already exploring this option on-line as the election results turned angry red across the map. Had I moved any distance at all away from our abuser, I would have lost custody of my young child and all legal right to see him without a supervisor. *Not Without My Daughter* and *Harvesting Stones,* are books about women caught in just such an impasse. *Crows Over a Wheatfield* by Paula Sharp is an award-winning fictionalized account of the underground railroad that exists for protective mothers who bravely attempt *flight* from a dangerous world turned upside down when all options to *fight* have been exhausted. Parents around the world do choose to leave their country of origin if violence there poses too grave a risk to their children. They flee out of protective love. For those of us who choose to stay here in the U.S. where the political system is clearly broken, a close look at some of the dynamics of the shattered family court system can offer lessons for framing the political debate for the next four years.

1. **Gender Bias is a Thing.** Think "The Taming of the Shrew." Mother dare not appear angry. Father may rant and rail. She must aim for "likable" while he will be deemed strong and determined for behaving like a raging bull. Her many past accomplishments will be called into question and scrutinized under the highest-powered microscope. His past failures will be reframed or ignored. His singular lack of qualifications to be a fit president/parent will be fully in evidence. Women may step forward to testify with credible allegations of physical and sexual assault and of emotional abuse.

   Maddeningly, it may not matter in the end. The validity of their claims and their motivation for coming forward will inevitably be questioned. My family law attorney submitted sworn affidavits from two former wives attesting to their experience of domestic violence with the man who had petitioned for full custody of our child. The circuit court judge refused to consider their testimony. His explanation was that,

234

in his experience, "ex-wives too often have an axe to grind." The outcome of the contest, the results of which will have life and death consequences for many, may hinge on the fact that certain men in positions of power didn't like the pantsuit "that bitch" wore to court/the debate. I learned too late that a protective mother should never wear a black suit (skirt, stockings and pumps notwithstanding) to family court. In the last courtroom, where my child's tragic fate was decided, the wall was lined with framed portraits of past presiding judges. A more stodgy, dour, depressing line-up of old white men would be hard to find. Except of course as past presidents of the United States. The Republican nominee for POTUS in 2016 has tapped into a source of fuel for his campaign that lay just below the polite surface of American society: the deep-seated anger of white male rage. Frustrated, as they have watched their boundless and unfounded claims to entitlement eroding over the past 50 years, they see in Hilary everything they despise (meaning everything they fear.) She's smart. She's calm. She won't be silenced. "Lock her up!" is the solution and final court order in too many contested custody cases where mother refuses to turn over her children to a known abuser or where she stands her ground in self-defense on their behalf. The ERA never became law. Women and children have no real constitutional rights.

2. **The Mask of Sanity is optional dress.** Although Trump's ever-changing inner circle of "advisors" and "managers" would prefer that he modify his behavior and speech so as to appear less unhinged, their lack of success does not mean that His Majesty the Baby may not prevail. Arrogance, grandiosity, vanity, a minimizing of past failings, a refusal to accept personal responsibility or to admit any fallibility — the hallmarks of narcissistic personality disorder — not only prohibit the diseased one from accepting any suggestion that

change might be advisable, they play well to the closeted narcissists who will give him a thumbs-up in his run for power. My son's father changed legal counsel as often as Trump has engaged and dismissed campaign managers. No one can exert client control over the pathological narcissist for long. Trump's vicious, personal attacks on his opponent in the debates rekindled terrible memories for me, as they have for countless women in the U.S. "There is hate in her heart." "She's a bully." She is a "nasty woman" and quite possibly aligned with the devil. He carries on, splitting and projecting his way to the top. Author Gail Sheehey, in an October article for *Politico* entitled *American Therapists Are Worried About Trump's Effects On Your Mental Health,"* observes this:

> It came up in the debate Sunday night, when Hillary Clinton pointed to a "Trump effect," an uptick in bullying and distress that teachers are noticing in classrooms as their students are exposed to a candidate who regularly attacks his opponents in bombastic, even threatening terms. The new revelation of Trump's crude boasts in 2005 about being able to kiss and grope women and 'move on' a married woman 'like a bitch' gave new fuel to the charge that his candidacy might be normalizing aggressive, disparaging talk and behavior.[29]

It doesn't matter what evidence turns up of women and children treated like objects. They were the pawns in this game all along. Consider the trophy wives and the children whom he paws in ways that make us all queasy. Video tape of the "man" behaving like a beast? Proof that he lied about having a foreign passport or about the number of children he sired? Evidence that he is a serial predator? Multiple convictions for international parental abduction or the fact that three of his male children have

29 www.politico.com/magazine/story/2016/10/donald-trump-2016-therapists

committed suicide? A lawsuit pending about the rape of a fourteen year old girl? Onward he sails to conquest.

3. **Doublespeak is Dangerous.** My mother was taught to say "Sticks and stones can break my bones but words will never hurt me." This is patently not true. Words have power, as my late friend, the theologian and author, Conrad Bonifazi, used to teach. Our words go out into the world and then work to recreate it. Words inspire others, tapping into powerful human urges for either love, connection and cooperation or for death and destruction. Hate speech on the airwaves in Rwanda served to incite civil war and to unleash genocide. Many bones were broken, bodies hacked to pieces, as a result. Already, Trump's bullying, racist and misogynist language has had a poisonous effect on the populace. Laura Basset, Senior Politics Reporter for *the Huffington Post* wrote a brilliant piece in October entitled, *"Donald Trump and His Supporters are Actually Making Women Sick, Including Me."* She writes, "Donald Trump and his bombastic, truth-free persona is still baffling to many. But for one select group of people — survivors of domestic violence — Trump is immediately and intimately recognizable. He reminds them of the men who ruined their lives."[30] It is no coincidence that at the very moment when the systematic disenfranchisement of people of color was being uncovered as a major social and political injustice in this country, Trump's campaign stepped up bogus claims about "voter fraud." In other words, the voices of witnesses to a well-documented and widespread discriminatory practice (seen in the purging of voter rolls, the failure to provide adequate polling places in districts of color, the rise of voter registration requirements that would prevent

---

30 http://www.huffingtonpost.com/entry/donald-trump-women-sick_us_5804d6ece4b0e8c198a8fb66

237

too many poor people from exercising their constitutional right to vote, etc.) were suddenly drowned out by louder voices echoing lies about undocumented voters and a Democratic party bent on skewing the results of our political process. The sheer temerity of such a ploy is mind-boggling, to say nothing of the fact that the media gives it play as though it were "a thing." Those of us who have been studying the crisis in our nation's family courts are familiar with this diabolical slight of hand. At the very moment when journalists, civil rights attorneys, and feminist scholars were beginning to shed a light on the plight of women and children facing their abusers in contested custody disputes, militant fathers' rights groups coined the term "Parental Alienation Syndrome." Like "voter fraud," this bogus diagnosis for a very real problem makes finding a cure suddenly less possible than ever. Burning witches did not cure the plague but it left many children motherless. The hypothesis that vindictive, hysterical women rush to fabricate stories of child abuse, intimate violence and incest as ways so separate their children from good fathers has been thoroughly debunked. Nevertheless, the equivalent of climate change deniers continue to rule from the bench in family court, accusing us protective mothers of malicious and even criminal behavior. Their judicial operating system has been infected with a deadly virus. As unscientific and fear-based propaganda is unleashed into public discourse, finding its way into the echo chambers owned by the privileged few, it poisons the water of our consciousness as surely as lead leaching into the pipes and public drinking water in Flint. In family court, as in Flint, children are the most vulnerable. It is they who are most likely to suffer lifelong damage as the result of the toxic behaviors, the cover-ups, the croneyism, the corruption of irresponsible adults.

4. **The Serial Litigator is also a Serial Abuser.** The guy who returns to court again and again and again does so at enormous expense to the Taxpayer. That's you and that's me. Yes, the individual players need to have enough personal assets or money raised from supporters to stay in the game. It's pay to play all the way. But there is also a great deal of money being made from this adversarial system which pits two players against each other, all in the name of "justice" and "equality." (Are we talking here about the national presidential "cycle" which runs 50% of the time in America, two years out of four, or about the family court system where a case may drag on for three, seven, ten years or longer? The answer is both.) He may be the guy who, according to USA Today has litigated in more than 4,000 cases over three decades." Trump uses the lawsuits to negotiate throughout his business relationships. He turns to litigation to distance himself from failing projects that relied on the Trump brand. And he uses the legal system to haggle over his property bills and contracts with vendors."[31] Or again, he may be the guy involved in family court disputes with four women over the custody of nine different children in two countries and in three different states over three decades. I can tell you about him or you can look him up. Perhaps lock him up? We are all paying the price for the rampages of unbridled Ego on an epic scale. The narcissist may try to project a persona of the strong man, but one has only to look at the record. He is constantly showing that he perceives himself as the wronged and wounded victim. He will return in an endless loop of litigation to the courts because he will always be able to pay a lawyer to tell him what he longs to hear, that he is right, that he has been wronged. He is ripping off all of us and like any true con he becomes more smug with each "success." He's smarter

---

31 http://www.usatoday.com/pages/interactives/trump-lawsuits/

than us all and tells us so. That's why he doesn't pay taxes and we do, he said. (And then denied that he said it.) In domestic violence circles, it's referred to as financial abuse. American taxpayers have been the unwitting victims of Trump's addiction to serial litigation, footing the bill for his use of our nation's courts to wage his private battles against his perceived enemies for years. A close look at the small percentage of custody disputes which become custody wars reveals a parallel universe worth exploring.

5. **It's a Mad Tea Party Once we've Fallen into the Rabbit's Hole.** Are you concerned about our children's safety, about their future, about your ability to care for them and to provide them a future with educational possibilities beyond a lifetime of being held prisoner to war and fear? Are you concerned about violence against women and about the fact that men with histories of criminal violence can easily access assault rifles? Were you hoping for a day in court (or in the debates) where you, and others whose lives are most likely to be effected by the final outcome, might hear these urgent matters addressed? Forget about it. The conversation will always come back to Himself, how he has been wronged, how everyone is out to get him. It's the narcissist's open wound speaking — or oozing. Against all odds, he will manage to hijack the debate. He will claim without any sense of irony that the very system into which he inserted himself as a contender has been rigged. There will be no more logical, reasonable discussion at the table. When asked by our court-appointed mediator whether he planned to pay me any of the $58,000 he owed me in court-ordered fees, my adversary said, "Not a dime!" And when asked for an explanation, he said, "I am responsible to a higher authority." To what higher authority was he

appealing, one can only wonder, when it was he who had taken our domestic affairs dispute to the Court of Appeals in the State of Oregon? Though I had prevailed in court, his own reality prevails because he wills it to be so. ***Trump will accept the outcome of the election in a few days on one condition, he says: only if he wins.*** When the pundits began to refer to this election cycle as a circus, the officials of Barnum and Bailey protested. A real circus requires that well-trained, skilled performers operate in an organized and cooperative effort. No law will be able to hold him accountable, this Mad Hater/Hatter. Though Hillary be six, seven or one hundred times exonerated for using a private e-mail server, he will come back to the issue and will continue to call her the criminal. Each time I hear T-rump say "Crooked Hillary" I recall something one of the psychologists involved in my late child's custody case remarked: "Think of 'the crooked little man in his crooked little house who lived there with his crooked little cat and his crooked little mouse' in the children's nursery rhyme. Anyone who enters his world will be expected to pretend not to notice that everything in his world is crooked. It's *his* distorted reality and he'll do anything to preserve it."

6. **Coercive Control Looks Like This.** It refuses to be seated though debate decorum demands it. It strides up to the Bench as *pro se* litigant and has to be reminded by the Judge that it doesn't belong there. It will circle, scowl, prowl, and growl — like a wolf stalking a lamb. It says, "I seize this moment to show you that I am on the move and I am closing in on you and everyone can see and no one can stop me." Ironically, Trump's vile and predatory treatment of women came spilling into view over the course of Domestic Violence Awareness Month. Melissa Jeltsen, another senior reporter with *the Huffington Post*, addressed coercive control in her piece, "*Trump is Triggering Domestic Violence Survivors with

241

Textbook Abusive Behavior. He lies. He bullies. He threatens. And he's one step away from the presidency." She notes that "While domestic abuse is often characterized as acts of violence, it's more accurate to understand it as a cluster of specific behavioral tactics that abusers employ to control, intimidate and coerce victims."[32] My adversary in the Custody Wars wanted to tail me down the courthouse steps after he lost the first lawsuit he filed against me. Having foreseen this, I had asked two male friends to accompany me and they provided a shield behind me so that his awfulness could not literally breathe down my neck. Too many women have been killed in retaliation after filing for separation, for a restraining order and for custody of the children, a sad fact I've learned from my work in the domestic violence community. Coercive Control is expert at making veiled threats, so murky that their intention can later be denied and yet so clear that when violence occurs, as it surely will, the handwriting on the wall will mock us and our refusal to see. It was written in blood. An unswerving and overwhelming desire to dominate is the essential driving force behind domestic violence, behind child abuse, and behind any sociopath's rise to power — whether his goal is to be dictator of a nation or tyrant ruling over a woman and her children as his abject subjects. Coercive control makes wild promises (to the women whom it hopes to ensnare; to children, sadly, in the case of custody disputes; to a childish populace, in the case of Trump) on which it can never deliver. It lies brazenly to achieve its ends. When called out for these things, it rages anew, castigating those who dare oppose it as being petty, as being deluded, or as being the ones who lie. Coercive control loves the chaos that results as all possibility for any

---

32 http://www.huffingtonpost.com/entry/donald-trump-is-triggering-domestic-violence-survivors-with-textbook-abusive-behavior_us

reasonable discussion is swept away in the storm it creates. Everyone wearies of what has become (very intentionally, make no mistake about it!) an interminable, exhausting, battle where no one can recall any longer the salient points. Everyone wants out. It's all too much and so it becomes easy and tempting to frame the entire debate and dispute as a matter of "he said - she said." The problem here being that, as Rebecca Solnit has noted, when a disagreement is framed as "he said-she said," it's always to discredit 'she said.'[33]

I have learned the hard way. This doesn't end well.

Asking mom and dad to come up with one thing they admire about the other fools no one. The system can pretend that it has the best interests of the children or the people at heart. The results may show otherwise.

---

33   Solnit, Rebecca. *Men Explain Things to Me.* Haymarket Books. 2015.

The Sunshine House

Michelle Plata

I actually had a pretty awesome run as a single mother.

When my son was six and his sister was still a newborn, I ended the abusive marriage that I had fought ten years to save. The afternoon he pinned me against the kitchen counter and threatened me for the last time, what I hadn't been able to do before suddenly became easy. My baby daughter was asleep in the next room. In that instant, feeling the countertop cut into my back and seeing the knives an arm's length away, I became my daughter. Someone was doing this to her. That can never happen. I would leave. For real this time.

My heart breaks a little knowing that I never drew that line for my son. Something shifted though when I had a daughter.

The next day I got a restraining order (not the first one I'd ever had) and a divorce lawyer (also not the first). My ex-husband is in the military so I called his command to report the incident. That was a hard thing to do because it could have jeopardized his career, which would have put me and the kids in an even more precarious position. The military keeps him in line, more or less, and affords him a steady income.

We were living overseas at the time. It took many weeks for the military to permit me and the kids to return to the USA. My daughter didn't have proof of American citizenship yet so we couldn't board a plane. No longer trapped at home, but still trapped in a foreign country.

It was one of those European countries with broad social safety nets. It might have been a pretty great place to be a single mother, but my visa did not entitle me to those benefits. Waiting for travel authorization gave me plenty of time to journal about all the ways we would be fucked when we got back to the USA: Childcare. Housing. Health insurance. Ticking through the list during a counseling session, my gracious local therapist attempted to soothe me, "Surely there are government programmes available to help single mums." I laughed.

The plane touched down in California. We didn't move back into our house, which would be sold in the divorce. We didn't live with my parents. We didn't go to a women's shelter. We stepped across the threshold of our new home and collapsed into the very bosom of the Goddess.

Through a series of miraculous connections, I rented us a cottage at *Shakti Rising*. You need to understand that *Shakti Rising* is two things. It is a social change organization that cultivates the health and emerging leadership of women and girls through a network of affiliated communities originating with its hub, "Sunshine House," in downtown San Diego. The expanded, witchier explanation is that it is also an alchemical journey wherein one's own inner healing and service to the world join together, ultimately empowering women to utilize their personal transformation as a catalyst for positive change in their families and communities. This actively promotes community well-being and creates woman- and child-friendly societies that are safe, healthy, vibrant, diverse, sustainable and culturally alive. Years earlier (ironically, when my marriage first showed signs of abuse), I became part of the *Shakti Rising* sisterhood and invoked the power of transformation to uncover, rediscover and reclaim my whole self. It was time to go back and peel away the next layer.

For the next two and a half years, I would mend my heart and raise my kids there.

We were a dozen women in three houses, all in various stages of glorious disrepair, the women and the houses both, linked by a shared yard and a call to live life better. There were Solstice celebrations with flower-filled piñatas. Sunday night dinners of produce from the garden. Ecstatic dance parties. Late nights spent laughing/crying on the kitchen floor. Rituals of grief and release. Heads were shaved. Murals painted. Divorces finalized. There were no men. It took my son a while to notice it was just him and the cat anchoring the masculine.

Each week, those of us who were elders in the community gathered for a Goddess Circle. We called on Hecate, Baba Yaga, Quan Yin, Yemaya, Mary, the Fairie Queen. She answered to so many names. Pieces of my soul returned to me: found in the attic, at the ocean's edge, along the labyrinth, around the fire. I had been scattered, yet She knew where each fragment lay and whispered clues to me. Bit by bit, I became myself again. One night, surrounded by my sisters on the journey, Her message was very clear: "LIVE THE LIFE THAT'S MEANT TO BE YOURS! You'll need to get some chickens."

I was getting good at making safe places for soft creatures to live, so I built a coop in that big shared yard and got three urban chickens.

Today I have 79 chickens... and also turkeys, ducks, pigs and sheep.

Perhaps it's obvious we don't live in downtown San Diego anymore. We live on a farm. In the northwest. A place I've dreamed of returning to since I lived here as a girl.

246

Living the life that was meant to be mine.

Yes, partly that's because I followed a divine call back to who I am. It's also partly because I couldn't afford to be a single mother in the big city. There came a point where I could no longer float some $20,000 in unpaid child support. In a beautiful collision of the sacred and the mundane, my dream of homesteading unfolded because I was too broke to stick with the path I was already on. I applied for jobs in rural areas, places with a lower cost of living. They made me offers. I had to turn some down. Why? Because offers have start dates and I couldn't get there on time. Legally I could not move my children out of the State of California without the written approval of their father (who had a history of abusive behavior, and who hadn't seen them in almost a year, and whose failure to pay court-ordered child support necessitated the move). The alternative was to go to court to request permission from a judge. That would take an unknown amount of time, maybe months, and would cost several thousand dollars. But I did it. I got the judge's signature, landed a job, moved away, and leased some land.

Raising my kids in community during our time at *Shakti Rising*, surrounded by loving surrogate-aunties and their children, was an incredible experience. It doesn't really seem accurate to call that chapter of my life "single motherhood" because I was not doing it alone, not hardly. We jokingly called each other "sister wives of the divine feminine." Really though, that was exactly what we were to each other and to Her. I miss those women fiercely. When I moved away from Sunshine House, Spirit sent me off with the message, "I know you're scared to leave the community you have here, but go! Your tribe will meet you there."

It's very quiet by comparison to now live with just one other adult, an incredible life partner. We're raising kids together, growing food

247

and dreaming about that village. I trust it is already taking shape. We're just the first residents is all.

Photo: The Sunshine House

Becoming My Own Midwife

Celeste Gurevich

I learned to survive by quilting myself with breath, blood, bones, and stories.

Panel by panel, saturated remnants of all of the Celestes I have ever been. The stitches laden with the scent of early Spring daphnes, garden-fresh basil a licorice-y labor of loving hands. The eternal tang of salty Pacific Ocean air. In the warp and weft of fiber, my scars, each with its own tale to tell.

Listen carefully and you will hear the music that moves me. You will feel the boiling momentum gathering in my root chakra, moving through my limbs with the notes, up through my arms and legs. The release, exquisite, of muscles moved to dance. Of vocal cords thrown open in song.

Mine is an embodied body. A body that was abused, and is still in recovery, rediscovery. A body that brought life into the world without a pharmaceutical fog to separate me from my Pain. A body that has walked barefoot, childtoes in love with mud-thick, warm Mother Earth juices.

Mine is a body in flux, at the mercy of the dialogue between estrogen and progesterone, the interplay of ovaries and uterus. A bodymachine heaving herself in fits and starts toward cronehood.

And I.
Am.
Ready.

Arms wide open to this New Self, it is time to embrace my failings, see them anew. To honor them as blessed teachers.

To reclaim.

From this day forward, I transmute into power being told that I should NOT read in class my very first day of school. Shamed by the adult in charge for teaching myself to read. The embarrassment, guilt for being smart at six years old.

As of today, I recognize my value in my relationships. Off with the blinders of self-doubt. I see now that I was a woman desperately in need of affection, for someone to have my back, to hold me and say it would be okay. Settling for abuse or safe mediocrity because I couldn't yet see that I could thrive, and not merely survive.

I reclaim my own experience of being a poor, struggling single mother in a generation of women who watched as socially guaranteed safety nets were yanked out from under our feet. Denying those of us who ached to elevate. Those of us who were willing to sacrifice, those of us who kicked and screamed against the System.

All we wanted was the opportunity to succeed.

I'll take every shitty job, every small-minded, small-dicked tyrant boss.

Decades of working my body to chronic pain and injury for someone else's profit.

I call to power my library and barstool education. I rose beyond the poor-ass school district I spent hard time in. Held my creativity close. Set my own curriculum. Pushed through being denied funding and support to continue my education. The thing I wanted most desperately.

I proclaim my diploma from The Global University of the Self-Educated and the Academy for the Ideal of Unlimited Potentiality. I claim it all.

Every piece invaluable. After all, until you fall enough, how can you lose your fear of falling?

It made me who I am today.

Healer, mother, writer, artist, empath, musician, wife, gourmet chef. Grandmother. Matriarch.

Holding the line of my ancestors. Holding the line.

Heart wide open.

Mind on fire.

There is wisdom, empathy and strength through suffering and pain. If you chose to look that motherfucker in the eye and not blink. To jump free-fall down into your stories is a courageous act, and they are the most crucial gift we have to give one another.

To say FUCK YOU to fear is the only way to create new trajectories for ourselves. Away from abuse. Away from neglect. Toward loving ourselves as we are. Knowledge, consciousness, and righteous outrage are my weapons.

Stretching, my mind and spirit are being pulled outward in every direction. Ocean size. To the nebulas. Far enough to hold the magnitude of abundance that is my life now. That is my love. Now.

Mind wide open. Heart on fire. Expanding, out and out and up and beyond, wide enough to hold all of the intensity and passion and pain and humanity and laughter and sex and joy and stories and stories and love and art.

I'm a Woman Transformed

Chris Ball

Now...

I'm a woman transformed.

Love + empathy + compassion + acceptance $>$ hate + fear + derision + manipulation

I'm a woman fed (and driven) by peace and calm. I'm strong and whole.

(and no amount of your shouting/blaming/hating/hitting /delaying/revenging tactics can take that from me.
You don't want to pay child support? OK!
You don't want to wash clothes? No problem!
You don't want to speak peacefully and with respect?
I can't change that, but you don't get to me anymore)

YOU'RE NO LONGER AN INFLUENCE IN MY LIFE. YOU ARE ONLY A SMALL, BUZZING FLY THAT ANNOYS ME FROM TIME TO TIME. YOU ONLY EVER GOT YOUR POWER FROM ME (you have no power) I CHOOSE NOT TO EMPOWER YOUR SAD, SORRY AND ABUSIVE BEHAVIOUR

I AM IN MY POWER AND I DON'T RECOGNISE YOU IN MY LIFE thank you for taking me on this journey of discovery. i am a bigger and better person than ever

In the beginning...

Pregnant. Contemplating choices. (Remember when it felt like you had choices?) (*get rid of it*). A booked abortion cancelled. Another one, cancelled. An emotional and heartbreaking spiritual ceremony to farewell this soul with a heartbeat, deeply embedded in me, feeling like a star-studded portal to the Universe and Its oneness (can't bring myself to say the words "goodbye"). A tear-drenched decision (not even a decision) to 'keep' that soul, and a commitment to do my best by it. All my heart-soul-being-energy transforming into love and joy and pouring into this new little baby inside.

(So innocent! No idea then, none, not even an inkling of an awareness!) of what a complex web of terror, manipulation, pursuit and fear-confusion-frustration-pain (so much pain) could be created and imposed. Sigh. Oh, to have that innocence back...). Erosion of self...

Small words: *"we can't afford that," "you need to work more," "if only you were different"* crept in around *"I love you and will never leave you,"* and the uncomfortable feeling-voice (pit of the stomach, such a loud clear message now, why (WHY!?) didn't I hear it then?), (mis)identified as: 'this man is vulnerable and seeks to feel validated'.

Back then, I was a strong woman, with love to spare and confidence to burn. In giving, I assumed your vulnerability would dissipate. You took my freely offered love and confidence. It didn't come back. And your 'vulnerability' got louder. (*So much shouting!*) More love given. (*Taken.*) Taken, and transformed... (*"you always ruin things," "why can't you see why you're to blame," "you think you're so great," "you won't ever change," "you need to change."*)

255

Envelopes of obsessive expressions of love enclosed hate-words, hate feelings. Inside me, a thorny, prickly, hard to explain, out of control, scrambled-eggs brain feeling (such a clear message NOW, but why (WHY!?) couldn't I understand it then?).

LOUD! (So loud!) **LOUDER!** (A broken chair). IT HURTS! (Dragged, screaming). LET ME OUT! (Where would you go? You can't leave me. I'll follow you wherever you go). **LET ME OUT!** (A blocked doorway, a raised fist). **BLACKNESS...............**

crying → confusion → trying → hoping → denial → crying (**SO LOUD!**) → resignation → crying

And then...

POLICE! (I need help to get him out!) thinking that I'll be free, that this will end, that your rage will stop. **SO WRONG. THINGS GOT SO MUCH WORSE. TWO WHOLE YEARS OF.......**

·Fear

·Disempowerment

· Bullying

· Vexatious (mis)use of the legal system

· Emotional abuse

· Financial abuse

· Vitriol

Exhaaaaaaaaaaaaaaaaaaaaaustion.....

You were stronger and more manipulative than I gave you credit for. You systematically took advantage of every organisation set up to protect against family violence. Your lies and manipulation led to: a Police family violence being order taken out against me; five court appearances (me as the respondent) in 12 months; me being unable to leave the state; me feeling emotionally exhausted and constantly concerned for the well-being of our incredibly resilient and lovely son.

But your abuse has led me to a better place. I am supported in sisterhood by many strong and passionate women. My son is growing into an emotionally sensitive and empathetic person. Your behaviour has led me to feminism, which enriches my life. I have changed my career and now dedicate myself to promoting peace and well-being. I have you to thank.

Without you, my life would have been more peaceful, but now I know the true value of peace.

Conclusion

Trista Hendren

We began this anthology a few weeks before Mother's Day in the United States. As someone who lived many years as a single mother, I had a few things to say.

So I began my blog post with these unpopular words...

Don't send me another fucking Mother's Day Card—or even flowers. **I want my back child support. That's right, all $33,201.04 of it.** If you love, value and appreciate mothers, spend this Sunday rallying for moms to get their child support payments—in full.

In the U.S. alone, that is more than $108 billion of unpaid support[34]—and *who pays*? Well, children obviously. But more than that, the mothers who care for them who do absolutely everything in their power—including sacrificing their own life, health and needs to make sure that their kids are taken care of.

I know this is an upsetting subject for some, because whenever I post about it, I get complaints saying that men sometimes don't get child support either. So here are some stats: 87% of custodial parents are women.[35] I don't want to go too far off tangent on the pay gap, but it is important to note that single mothers also make

---

34 Hargreaves, Steve. "Deadbeat parents cost taxpayers $53 billion." *CNN/Money*. November 5, 2012.
35 Casey, Timothy and Maldonado, Maldonado. "WORST OFF – SINGLE-PARENT FAMILIES IN THE UNITED STATES: *A Cross-National Comparison of Single Parenthood in the U.S. and Sixteen Other High-Income Countries* Legal Momentum: The Woman's Legal Defense and Education Fund. December 2012.

less[36] than other mothers, and certainly less than other men or even single fathers. Single dads have the entire world rooting for them. Single moms get treated like second-class citizens day-in and day-out. If you don't believe me, check out this[37], this[38] and this[39]—and then tell me that any of this would be "newsworthy" if it were about a single mom.

Today we are talking about Mothers. On Father's Day I will probably still be talking about mothers because for most of my children's lives, I have had to play both roles with very little financial support. And I know damned well I am not the only one.

Wouldn't it be wonderful if men who owed back child support couldn't go out and make new luxury purchases? I mean, what if a man who owed back child support went in to pay cash for the newest iPhone or car, and the sales clerk had to look him up in a registry first. Imagine the look on daddy's face when the clerk takes his money and tells him, "I'm sorry sir, but it looks like this will be going toward taking care of your children *first*."

It would be hard to enforce on dinners out and fancy new clothes, but as a single mom who rarely experienced either of those things, I think that sometime before next Mother's Day, the world could give us a real 'thank you' by at least making an effort.

---

36 Casey, Timothy and Maldonado, Maldonado. "WORST OFF – SINGLE-PARENT FAMILIES IN THE UNITED STATES: *A Cross-National Comparison of Single Parenthood in the U.S. and Sixteen Other High-Income Countries* Legal Momentum: The Woman's Legal Defense and Education Fund. December 2012.
37 Arata, Emily. "Single Dad Goes To Beauty School To Learn To Braid Daughter's Hair." *Elite Daly.* February 4, 2015.
38 Flaherty, Ciara. "Single dad and little daughter out for Valentine's Day receive heart-warming note from couple." *Breaking News.* February 17, 2015.
39 Mordecai, Adam. "This daddy-daughter hair-braiding class is heart-explodingly adorable." *Upworthy.* April 18, 2016.

When men don't pay child support, mothers are put into a situation where they can't pay their utilities, rent or even buy food. That means that utilities are shut off, families are evicted and children don't eat. Mothers don't get the doctor, dentist or any other treatments they need. Sometimes children don't *either*. The men who cause this should be the ones facing consequences.

There is a common argument that men should not be jailed for non-payment of child support. But **not feeding your children *is* abuse.**

Mothers who cannot feed their children are charged with child abuse or neglect. When you put the significant pay gap into play with the amount of mothers who do not receive child support, it is not a pretty picture for children. It is not healthy for children to grow up in chronic stress and poverty. **Non-payment of child support should be criminally prosecuted as child abuse.**

In most states, there are very few penalties for not paying child support on time or at all. It seems nothing much has changed in the decades since June Jordan wrote:

> *"At any rate, as my lawyer explained, the law then was the same as the law today; the courts would surely award me a reasonable amount of the father's income as child support, but the courts would also insist that they could not enforce their own decree. In other words, according to the law, what a father owes to his child is not serious compared to what a man owes to the bank for a car, or a vacation."*

$108 billion in unpaid support says child support enforcement is not working in the United States. We need to find places where these programs *do* work and ensure that children get the support that they need.

I wish I could say I received that back child support since I started writing about it, but my past due child support has now grown to more than $46,000.

As we were about to release this book, my children's father died unexpectedly. It was a very hard time for all of us, and perhaps the subject of another book.

Time will tell if my children ever see their past due child support— but I now know that it was always there, as I suspected, hidden in plain sight by someone who claimed to care about them.

I know I am not alone in struggling to raise my children without the financial support they need—and after reading this anthology, so do you.

In what sort of a civilized world do you allow children not to be taken care of by *both* their parents? In what sort of world can men not pay for their house and car and continue to drive and live in them? Why are there not more sanctions for not paying child support? More than $108 billion is not a *small* problem. And it doesn't begin to measure the long-term effects on women and children.

One has to wonder if denying children and mothers financial support is POLICY at this point. This is not rocket science. Some States collect child support significantly better than others. Nordic countries are about as good as it gets.[40] It is time for the world to

---

40 Casey, Timothy and Maldonado, Maldonado. "WORST OFF – SINGLE-PARENT FAMILIES IN THE UNITED STATES: *A Cross-National Comparison of Single*

learn from what *is* working and rise up and demand better for women and children.

> *"We reject the patriarchal, androcentric, and capitalist value system which labels caring as worthless, demeaning, and inferior, and we reject the patriarchal model of family. We promote the truth about mothering; that it is strength, power, resilience, and requires endurance, skill, creativity and self-mastery. We believe that the negative way mothering, as 'women's work', is viewed and treated in our society is symbolic of the way in which all women's work is viewed and treated. We insist that mothering be acknowledged as real work, and we call for the introduction of Basic Income to reflect this (as well as destigmatising benefits in general). We believe in the rights of children as full, equal beings, their right to their mothers, and their right to vital attachment and loving, safe, free, innocent, explorative childhoods, free of poverty, abuse, sexualisation, gender stereotyping and adult stresses." -Esther Parry, All Mothers Work*

Even if you just have five minutes to do something, take a moment and write to the National Child Support Office at OCSEHotline@acf.hhs.gov to demand change. Read the "Call to Action" chapter that follows and join us in creating change.

Post and share about this issue on social media. Non-payment of child support and financial abuse are feminist issues—and they deserve more coverage.

Parenthood in the U.S. and Sixteen Other High-Income Countries
Legal Momentum: The Woman's Legal Defense and Education Fund. December 2012.

For the single mothers who are tired beyond what they can bear. For the single mothers working three jobs who never see the children they are trying so desperately to raise. For the single moms who watch their ex-husbands show up in Gucci loafers every week while their children don't have enough food. For the single mothers who have to marry tyrants (again) to pay the bills. For the single mothers whose children have been sucked up by the "Family Court" industry. For the single mothers who are laid up in hospital beds after stress-induced heart attacks—while their ex-partners are "too tired" to bring their children to their beds. For the single mothers who have lost—or nearly lost—their children to suicide. For the single moms who have to leave their daughters elsewhere for years at a time to ensure them a better future. For the single mothers who are raped or killed by ex "partners," who don't scream or fight—because their children would hear. For every single mom out there who has killed herself (literally, or not quite) so that her children can have what they need.

We stand with you and shout:

WE ARE DONE WITH THIS BULLSHIT.

Single mothers and our children deserve better.

Women of the world, rise up and join your sisters in demanding better.

Call To Action

Trista Hendren

One question that repeatedly came up during the compilation of this anthology was: **What can I do to help?**

I have given this question a great deal of thought, and also posted it to the other contributors. The first thing I'd like to share is some personal experiences that made the biggest difference in my life and that of my children.

Single moms often need help in the practical, every day sense. I want to share this first because it's something every person can do now that will help immediately while we wait for the systematic change that needs to happen.

My mother and co-editor probably saved my life. I am not sure I could have made it through my years as a single mom without her help. When she saw that I was alone, she told me, "Consider me your partner in raising your kids."

This gave me the freedom to ask for what I needed from her without feeling guilty. If I needed help getting the kids to school, or navigating between various appointments and school functions —she was there. She took the kids on a regular schedule so I could work or have time to myself. The last years before we moved to Norway, we all lived together. Having another adult in the house with young children helped tremendously. Not to mention, if it were not for my mother's financial support, I would have been homeless—with my children—numerous times.

When my children's father died suddenly, we were not even remotely in a position to come home—although I knew almost immediately that we needed to. My longtime friend Daylene offered to set up a GoFundMe for us—which ultimately enabled us to take the trip.

I am a very proud person, so putting this out there was very difficult for me. My heartfelt gratitude to Daylene for putting it together and all those who contributed to the fund.

In my early years as a single mom, the Spaccarelli family in Lake Oswego invited us on their annual camp out at Orcas Island. This is a trip that I never could have pulled off on my own and one that none of us will ever forget. They had been taking this trip as a family for 40 years and had all all the camping, canoeing and fishing equipment imaginable. And, if you are familiar with Riccardo's Ristorante, you *know* how well we ate.

When we moved to the St. John's neighborhood, we had awesome neighbors. This allowed me to homeschool my daughter with support from her best friend's mom across the street. It also meant that we had handy men around who helped me assemble benches without being asked, hauled the heavy furniture and did whatever else I couldn't manage on my own.

Lastly, there are a few extraordinary men in this world who I would like to also recognize and thank. My first husband, Hussein, lent me money numerous times—no questions asked—the first year of my son's life. He also was a wonderful source of emotional support and has served as an honorary uncle to both of my children.

My current husband, Anders, has done more for my kids and I than I can ever repay. There were numerous weeks before we moved to Norway where he ate nothing but oatmeal so that my children could eat and I could pay the rent. He has put up with all shades of crazy over the last 5+ years without complaint—and has become the father that my children lacked. His belief in me—and the work that I do—has allowed me to heal and continue on with The Girl God books.

Aside from the personal help that I received, I think it is important for us to **think big.** Single mothers have been a low priority for too long. It is time to demand child support enforcement everywhere.

If you are in the U.S., contact your state child support office and ask them to make enforcement a priority. Contact your senators and governor and do the same. Remind them that $108 billion dollars is a lot of money to go uncollected with serious repercussions for women and children.

I have already mentioned the National Support Office. Take a moment to write and tell them to start enforcing child support. (OCSEHotline@acf.hhs.gov.) As I have written to them numerous times: *"Why even have an office of "Child Support Enforcement" if you don't enforce anything?"*

If you are outside the U.S., take a moment to get acquainted with how child support is collected and enforced in your country. Talk to single moms and ask them if their needs are being met. If you can help with some of those needs, please do. And please, join those of us who have lived as single moms in demanding change.

> "As feminists, we must start to demand that our political and economic systems live up to our dreams, for ourselves

and our children. The fact that we don't is a telling demonstration of that old chestnut: we are silenced out of fear or shame, of not wanting to want too much, not wanting to demand or expect, lest we overstep our mark. Thing is, if we don't speak up, if we don't demand the political system reflect rather than dictate, nothing is going to improve." -Vanessa Olorenshaw[41]

Lastly, be sure to check out the Single Mothers Discount Card, which was launched in 2021. The Single Mothers Discount Card is a grass-roots company created to advance social justice, particularly to advance women's rights in the realm of the family. Simply put, the SMDCard is designed to help single moms and businesses partner up to help each other do better.

41 Orenshaw, Vanessa. *Liberating Motherhood: Birthing the Purplestockings Movement.* Womancraft Publishing. 2016.

Single moms can join for free. If you have a business, you can support this initiative by signing up as a partner. https://www.singlemothersdiscountcard.com/

We will continue to add links to petitions and other updated action steps on my website: http://thegirlgod.com/singlemothers.php

Thank you in advance for your part creating radical change.

List of Contributors

Trista Hendren (editor and contributor) founded Girl God Books in 2011 to support a necessary unraveling of the patriarchal world view of divinity. Her first book—*The Girl God*, a children's picture book—was a response to her own daughter's inability to see herself reflected in God. Since then, she has published more than 40 books by a dozen women from across the globe with help from her family and friends. Originally from Portland, Oregon, she now lives in Bergen, Norway. You can learn more about her projects at www.thegirlgod.com.

Pat Daly (editor) is a mother of three daughters and proud grandma. A published author / writer on career and job search issues, Pat lives in Portland, Oregon. She has edited all of the Girl God books from the beginning.

Liz Darling (cover artist and contributor) is a visual artist living and working in Pittsburg, KS. She completed her BFA at Pittsburg State University in 2010. Deliberate and intricate, Darling creates precise compositions that often center on themes of spirituality, transience, the divine feminine, and the natural world.

Beth Mattson mothers, teaches, writes, bakes, fawns over a vegetable garden, and fights the patriarchy tooth and nail in the Driftless Region of Wisconsin.

Kelsey N. Lueptow has a Masters in creative writing and pedagogy from Northern Michigan University and is pursuing a Masters in literature at Marquette University. She has contributed to Everyday Feminism and Diary of a First Time Mom. She has published pieces in Red Paint Hill, Pidgeonholes, The Wisconsin Calendar of Poets 2015, and East Coast Literary Review, among other beautiful journals. These essays are part of her creative writing thesis, which threads researched academic essays, creative nonfiction essays, and poetry about the politics of motherhood in a braided form.

Jennifer Kimmel is writer and mother of three wonderful children. She currently resides in a tiny magical town on the top northwest tip of Ireland, and hopes to stay there for the remainder of her days. She enjoys hugging and reading to her kids, pairing mismatched socks, pretending sheep next door are mocking her hairstyle and experimenting with her new waffle maker.

Louise Pennington is a feminist writer and activist who works for the campaign organisation Everyday Victim Blaming, which challenges media misrepresentations of domestic and sexual violence and abuse.

Lucía Martínez is a Chicana Lesbiana visual artist from la Frontera of El Paso. Currently she's collaborating with the poet Jessica Ruizquez. Lucia Martinez's work has been exhibited throughout the Southwest and México and published in Mujeres De Maíz. Lucia has a BA in Art and Spanish and is currently a translator.

Jessica Ruizquez is a Chicana Lesbiana Mexica mama. Living and raising her baby, Paz Nican Tlacatl, in the traditions of their ancestors on the frontera of El Paso and Juarez. She has been a single, stay at home mama since giving birth to her son eight years ago. She is a hustler. Jessica earned her MA in Interdisciplinary Studies from UTEP where she studied "Curanderas of the Borderlands."

Solana Simpson is an artist and musician. She works as a teacher at a school with an awesome, alternative educational paradigm.

Throughout her life, she has been a midwife's apprentice, a seamstress, a singer in a traveling gospel group, twice a wife, a knitting and toy designer for a magazine, and most importantly, a mother to four wonderful children. Right now, she is pursuing her degree in psychology with a minor in creative writing. Since she has led a blessedly unconventional life, she is just now getting around to completing her degree. Solana is committed to her own inner work and using the voice of her experiences to help heal wounds unique to women; wounds having to do with parents, partners, culture, history, and society. She blogs at psycholobitch.com

Already an expert on how not to live life, **Nicola O'Hanlon** is a constant seeker of new and better ways of being. It is through seeking the Divine Feminine internally that she has been able to recover from the suppression of her own spirit. She is a believer in the power of magic, nature, energy healing, crystals and blames the phases of the moon for her multi personalities. She is Editor-In-Chief of www.iloverecovery.com, a new online publication for people in recovery from addiction and mental health issues, who want to express their own journey through all forms of the Arts. Her own work is widely published in several recovery magazines, including Recovery Today, In Recovery Magazine, and AfterPartyChat.com to name but a few. Her passion is to help people discover that wellness starts with self-empowerment.

Arna Baartz is a painter, writer/poet, martial artist, educator and mother to eight fantastic children. She has been expressing herself creatively for 44 years and finds it to be her favourite way of exploring her inner being enough to evolve positively in an externally focused world. Arna's artistic and literary expression is her creative perspective of the stories she observes playing out around her. Claims to fame: Arna has been selected for major art prizes and won a number of awards, published books and (her

271

favourite) was used as a 'paintbrush' at the age of two by well known Australian artist John Olsen. Arna lives and works from her bush studio in the Northern Rivers, NSW Australia. Her website is www.artofkundalini.com.

Colleen Joy Miller is a working artist and writer in Austin, Texas. She has two parrots and a challenging past of rape and miscarriage. Ms. Miller enjoys volunteering as an advocate for survivors of narcissistic abuse. She is passionate about gender equality, parrot linguistics, art, music, puppetry and mental health.

Susannah Gregan was born in Zambia in 1967. Her mother is Zimbabwean; her father is a white Australian. She moved to Australia in 1975 and has lived in Melbourne since 1987. In 1992 she gave birth at home to her only child: a son named Shaye. She raised him as a single mother. Once upon a time, she wrote a lot of poetry, did some theatre performance and went to art school. Susannah is a Black radical liberationist womanist feminist. She currently lives as a recluse.

Louise M Hewett is a Mother-Caregiver, Artist-Writer, Feminist and Priestess of Goddess, simultaneously, without hierarchy. She has been involved with Pagan and Goddess spirituality for more than twenty five years, expressing her experiences of unlearning and re-membering in ceremony, art, writing, and song lyrics, and has recently self-published her first novel, *Mist*. Louise lives in Strathalbyn, South Australia with three of her four children and is currently pursuing a Bachelor of Visual Art degree at Adelaide Central School of Art.

Marianne Evans-Lombe is a visual and performance artist. She creates body drawings. With her hand, she makes marks on paper, canvas, acetate, clay, and other materials. With her body, she gives movement to line, shape, words, and images. Her performances are grounded in mark making and her drawings are grounded in motion. Marianne holds a BFA and an MA in Visual Art from Pittsburg State University. She is an artist mama or a mama artist depending on the day. She is an activist in both her work and her personal life. She currently resides in Tulsa, Oklahoma.

Nile Pierce is a writer, artist, and proud single mother currently living and working in the United Kingdom. She is a member of Women's Liberation Front (WoLF) and a contributing radio-host on Women's Liberation Radio News. You an also find her social commentary on magnadea.org. If you are interested in changing the world with Nile and you would like to get in on a radical feminist non-profit organization focusing on single motherhood and all of the challenges therein, please contact her at contact@magnadea.org

Mia Wright is a native of Tulsa, OK, where she teaches high school English. Wright earned her MFA in Poetry from Boise State University. Her poems have appeared in Word Riot, Watershed, This Land, Living Arts of Tulsa's Kubos-Tesseract 40th Anniversary Chapbook, J'Parle' and countless restaurant napkins. She is also the author of three chapbooks: *Black Pussy* (2004), *prayers of calcitrant* (2010) and *Imaginary Lovers* (2013). Like most single mothers, Wright enjoys naps, wine, and getting stuff in the mail that isn't bills.

Jacinda Townsend is the author of *Saint Monkey* (Norton, 2014), which is set in 1950's Eastern Kentucky and won the Janet Heidinger Kafka Prize and the James Fenimore Cooper Prize for historical fiction. *Saint Monkey* was also the 2015 Honor Book of

273

the Black Caucus of the American Library Association, and was longlisted for the Flaherty-Dunnan First Novel Prize and shortlisted for the Crook's Corner Book Prize. Jacinda teaches in the Creative Writing Program at University of California, Davis, and is mom to two beautiful children who amaze her daily.

Lesley 'Orion' Johnson is a forest Valkyrie from upstate New York, the Finger Lakes region of the Oneida & Onondaga people. The youngest of eight children, Orion joined the military due to economic reasons out of high school and became a Mental Health Technician for seven years. She served in Missouri, Texas and South Carolina working in most genres of mental health primarily focusing on PTSD treatment. She developed a complex lens for interpreting and integrating how our culture approaches emotional wellness. After her service, Orion shifted her trajectory attending college, working in non-profit around anti-oppression dynamics and grassroots organizing in anti-police brutality, prisoner support work & solidarity with native and undocumented folks in Colorado. She also organized collective houses to facilitate communal emotional wellness networks. She is a mother of a fella named Jordan and she moved from city environments to raising her little one with the wild places. She has explored wilderness from Colorado to Northern California and Southern Oregon. Orion deeply values the wisdom of the land and her innate femme-ness. Currently she roams settler occupied 'Oregon' & 'Northern California' researching wild foods, class dynamics, concepts of shelter and wealth and the impact of settler people on indigenous culture. Orion is a poet and a visual artist and she focuses her art on honoring the feminine and conveying the contrast between the wild and civilization.

Orion witnesses her body as a map of the land and navigates her work from that place. She is guided by wild mushrooms and the seasonal cycle of processing acorns. She reinvents ownership with exosexual tenacity. She views our species as capable of harmony in the circle of life. She is a huntress of cosmic intuition and blunt realness. Her diet & physical health routine is survival on the fringes of capitalism.

Patty Kay is a retired bookkeeper in Lake Charles, Louisiana. She has studied ecology and world religions for the past forty years. Retirement has offered her the opportunity to delve further in her interests.

Auriol Hays is no mere musician. She is a Musical Storyteller, the village witch, a sonorous shaman beckoning all...

Multiple accolades aside, live is where this chanteuse captivates. Be it at the Montreux Jazz Festival in Switzerland, opening with the Gauteng Big Band at the Standard Bank Joy of Jazz, the Grahamstown National Arts Festival, Zoo Lake Music Festival, Suidoosterfees, Lusito Land Festival, the Folk and Acoustic festival or the Cape Town International Jazz Festival alongside the Brand New Heavies, Buena Vista Social Club and Jill Scott.

Socially conscious, Ms. Hays' Dreaming Music also includes a nod in support of Greenpeace, a song penned for the Arctic 30 titled "Come Home to Me," intended to highlight the plight of Arctic drilling in Russia and the impact on the environment.

Auriol is the proud brand ambassador for two NGO's – Help2read, dedicated to child literacy and Masikhule Child, who assists in educating and developing the needs of both women and children within marginalised communities.

She's also a board member of an innovative and cutting edge dance company, Dark Room Contemporary. 2015 saw Ms Hays nominated for an Mbokdo Women in Jazz award. In addition she released her deep house album, DeepHays, with DJ Rowick Deep.

Shamecca Long is a writer and spoken word artist from Brooklyn, NY. Her work has been featured in SIMBAA, The Abuela Stories Project, thelastwomensmagazine.com, GhettoHeat, Caribbean Life news, and blackcitymag.com. She is currently working on her second manuscript. Shamecca Long can be reached at shamecca.long@gmail.com.

Anne Bonnie has lived the last 13 years in Berlin. She was raised in a small Catholic town surrounded by a river, agricultural field, Trainrails and little forests. She lost her first child at 16 during an emergency operation in the seventh month of pregnancy. She gave birth to her children at 18 and 21 years, who have been raised by her ex-husband since they divorced.

Anne moved 500km away to Berlin to make up her A Level (Abitur). She got in touch in Berlin with occupied houses, anarchist and left theories. There she became a feminist and later a queer feminist. She founded the alternative Sexshop, Other Nature, in 2009 with a business partner. The shop has successfully been run by her ex-business partner since then. She is currently under apprenticeship to become a sex therapist.

In 2015 Annie became the mother of a black boy. Although she always anti-racist, she is now I learning about white privilege.

Irene Monica Sanchez is a Xicana, Single Mama, Artist, Writer, and Ph.D. Her writings have been published in Telesur and will be featured in an upcoming anthology titled "Basta! 100+ Latinas Against Gender Violence." She was a featured poet in the City of Seattle's Poetry on Busses Campaign called "Writing Home" in

2015 and a featured poet at the Latina/o Education Advocacy Days (LEAD) at CSUSB in 2016. Irene is determined to continue to cultivate and collaborate on artistic social justice projects while working full time and being a single mama full time. She speaks at colleges and universities and leads workshops relating to identity,

motherhood, and navigating institutions of higher education as a Woman of Color.

Irene began her "higher" education journey at Riverside Community College where she was placed on academic probation and dismissal her first year. Knowing the odds were stacked against her, she returned to school and transferred after five years to UC Santa Cruz where she completed her Bachelors degree in Sociology and Latin American/Latino Studies. She completed her Ph.D. and M.Ed. at the University of Washington-Seattle in Education Leadership and Policy Studies. She also holds a graduate certificate in Feminist Studies. Irene is a long time community activist focusing on women's empowerment, youth empowerment and immigrant/human rights. Originally born/from Southeast Los Angeles and raised primarily in the Inland Empire, she resides in the IE again where she works as a coordinator for an academic program at a community college. To connect with Irene see www.irenesanchezphd.com or find her twitter or instagram @irenemonicas

Veronica Cioaric is from the Republic of Moldova and is 32 years old. She does business development for an executive search company and has a Bachelor of Arts degree.

Kali Sunna is a dedicated mother of two beautiful children, and woman-positive freethinker. She has battled an abusive narcissist in three court jurisdictions and four courts with half a dozen judges and approximately 14 attorneys involved so far, in Southwestern VA, over the span of six+ years, in an effort to keep the children mentally and physically safe. Unfortunately, the court system supports the abuse and continues to frustrate her in her attempts at protecting the children's well-being; choosing instead to prioritize parental rights to visitation regardless of harm to children.

Martina Robles Gallegos came from Mexico as a teenager and lived in Altadena and Pasadena through high school. She then moved to Oxnard and attended community college. She transferred to California State University, Northridge and got her teaching credential. She taught for almost 18 years in Hueneme Elementary School District until a work injury followed by a stroke kept her home. Martina paused my Master's but resumed after hospitalization. She graduated with her M.A. June 2015. Works have appeared in Altadena Review, Nation Poetry, Hometown Pasadena, and Allpoetry. facebook.com/martina.gallegos.188

Destiny Eve Pifer is a self published author whose work has been featured in *Spotlight on Recovery, FATE Magazine, Redbook* and *True Confessions.* She is currently a news reporter for her local newspaper, *The Punxsutawney Spirit.* She is a single mom with a wonderful little boy named Dartanyan.

Brenna Jean Richart is a creative writing, sociology student at The Evergreen State College raising Luke; an eight year old Lego freak who has all the powers and can never ever die. They like to play with their main squeeze Grey Greg the cat and their queen bee Sula Rey the shep shep. Find out more on Instagram: @mamabearb88

Lennée Reid is a geeky veganish universalist witch doctor mama bear poet activist survivor goddess on the spectrum who doesnt like labels that uses punctuation when she d@mn well pleases smile emoticon period She is trying to make sense of it all and find peace. In addition to many chapbooks, Lennée was published in the UPS DIRT! project, Creative Colloquy, and her poems and photos are often in "Works In Progress." Lennée repped Olympia Peoples Mic in NYC for WOWPS 2016, has featured and slammed across the country, and was heard on the KAOS 89.3 lit show "Tell It Slant." Hear her revolutionary poetry at protests, marches, and vigils where Lennée speaks for the trees and calls bullsh!t, while advocating spiritual harmony. Lennée loves organic fair trade anything, road trips, karaoke, and random synchronicities. Namaste. Find her @lenneereid mamamystic.wordpress.com

Jakki McIntosh is a 30-year-old single mother of 3 girls who are budding feminists. Aside from being a full-time mother and holding down a full-time job, she is also a college student. Thrust into a world ruled by patriarchy and laden misogyny, she navigates life the best she can while rearing her children and working to empower women.

A.L. Hayes was born and raised in a working class area of Dublin, Ireland. Having worked in office administration for many years, she returned to university as a mature student and single mother, obtaining a BA in Psychology. Following a bad car accident in 2014 she decided to return to her teenage pursuits of writing and painting. Ms Hayes has only just begun to put her work into the public domain and has read some of her poems and short stories at public events. One of her greatest passions in life is animal welfare. She has volunteered for animal rescues and donated prizes of Pet Portraits to be auctioned to raise funds to care for abandoned pets.

LuLu is a pen name for a clinical and forensic psychologist, who is also an author and educator. She devotes her time to infusing K12 education with empathy and compassion. LuLu has three teenaged kids whom she homeschooled for several years while launching a non-profit organization serving educators, clinicians, parents, and teens globally. Her kids are also her collaborators, and bring joy and love to every moment. LuLu is married to her best friend, lover, and partner in business and life.

Shareen is 29 years old and lives in San Antonio, TX. As of 2016, she is making a career in the insurance industry and is enjoying being a single mother!

Elmira Rodriguez is a rising spirit. A soul dreamer, heart listener, and tree speaker. Moon, earth, water, and fire spellbound. A wounded, phoenixing, cancerian mama. A friend, and beautiful, phenomenal woomyn.

She lives at the social intersections of: Queer, woomyn, witch, mama, suicide survivor, orphan, survivor of interpersonal violence, C-PTSD diagnosed, intersectional feminist, academic, writer, white privilege, member of the underclass.

Julie Wolfrum, a single Mama living in the Rocky Mountains, loves adventuring with her trusty half alien, half human son, Z. She also explores the cosmos and offers guidance to willing souls through Astrology and Tarot. When not looking toward the sky, Julie, a professionally trained dancer, teaches children and adults a variety of movement styles giving sincere focus to authenticity and the highest of vibrations.

Noelle Williams was born in 1974 in Toronto, Ontario (Canada). First born and only daughter of three children. Widowed 13 years ago and single mother to two now grown children. The poem

"Flower Child" was written for her daughter regarding being a teen mother and the commitment and joy she felt of her impending birth. Noelle is a strong individual who has had varied life experiences. She has overcome and risen above all obstacles life has set on her path.

Educator, life-coach, mentor and expat entrepreneur (momtreprenuer), **Sierra Melcher** runs a small yoga studio in Medellin, Colombia. Writer, avid traveler and single parent, she specializes in community building, self-care and personal development. Sierra offers online mentoring for expats, entrepreneurs, educators and anyone seeking deeper knowledge of self.

Molly Pennington is a writer, a mentor, a speaker, a wife and a mother, and a lover of insight and whimsy. Her default setting is perpetual cheer, but she doesn't shy away from the wounds of the world. To Molly, nothing is more vital than social justice. She believes that perception and compassion are curative. Molly is here to make the world a little less mean. Instead: smarter, brighter, better. You can find out more about her at www.mollypennington.com.

Karen McLaughlin is a homeschooling mother, writer and singer from Northern Ireland, currently flying her kite in the winds of Donegal. She enjoys mooning the patriarchy, conversing with trees and spending quality time with her very needy sofa.

Leslie has worked in the non-profit sector for over ten years, focusing on integrating youth and social technologies to impact social renewal. She has served as a community facilitator on complexity issues, and lived and worked in a Camphill community supporting young adults with special needs and abilities. Now, when not raising her daughter and playing with friends, Leslie serves as a high school counselor, and in her personal time helps to coordinate massive multiplayer simulation game events (megagames) up and down the US West Coast in an effort to facilitate in-person, community-building activities that evoke the imagination and provoke people to action.

Katherine Belliel is an American writer based in Izmit, Turkey. With roots in Grand Rapids, Michigan and Columbus, Ohio, this Midwest native turned global citizen has a B.S in History and Religion from Eastern Michigan University. Her work has appeared in the expat anthologies *Tales from the Expat Harem* (Ashman and Gokmen, 2005) and Encounters with the Middle East (Bowman and Khashan, 2006). In addition to writing a weekly column for the English language, Istanbul-based daily Today's Zaman under the pen name "Elle Loftis," Katherine spends her time globe-trotting with her young son and caring for the neighborhood cats. She is currently co-editor of the soon-to-be published foodoir anthology *Sofra: A Gathering of Foreign Voices Around the Turkish Table* and is finishing her first historical fiction novel. Follow her on Twitter: @KatieBelliel

Ihla Nation has been a freelance writer for 20 years with 30 articles, essays, commentaries and reviews published in newspapers, magazines, anthologies, and online publications. She has a BA in Social Work and an MA in Religious Studies/Eastern Religions. She is retired as a result of health issues, but has never retired from single parenting. She lives in Boulder, Colorado.

Rhonda Case (www.freeasthesun.com) Associate Faculty, College of the Redwoods; 2015-16 Survivor Representative to the Management Team of the Family Court Enhancement Project in Multnomah County, Oregon (a project funded by the DOJ and Office of Violence Against Women) and Portland Liaison for Dr. Riane Eisler's Spiritual Alliance to Stop Intimate Violence (a project of the Center for Partnership Studies). www.saiv.org

Michelle Plata is living the life that's meant to be hers in Oregon, where she works in food security and community health. The original San Diego chickens – Calm, Brave and Twinkle-Twinkle – are doing well and enjoyed their stay at Motel 6 when the family moved. Visit shaktirising.org to learn more.

Celeste Gurevich is a multi-medium Social Artist, Bird Nerd and proud Matriarch who grew up on the Central Oregon Coast, and has lived in Portland for almost 25 years. Her work has been published in *Perceptions: A Magazine for the Arts, The Manifest-Station,* and elsewhere. She is also an Associate Producer of the podcast, *On The Block Radio.*

Celeste is currently putting together her first chapbook of poetry. If you need more of her words, you can find her on all the social medias.

Chris Ball is a gypsy woman who found peace in adventure, and now finds adventure in peace. Environmental conservation featured heavily in her early career, and she now facilitates physical and emotional transformations through peaceful and restorative floatation therapy. Her son is her constant reminder to be slower, better, more aware and more grateful. She is.

If you have valued this book, please consider writing a brief review on Amazon and/or Goodreads.

This book is offered freely as a PDF to any woman who is (or was) a single mom who is struggling financially.

There is a link on my website:
http://thegirlgod.com/singlemothers.php

Made in the USA
Monee, IL
15 March 2022

92422329R00177